Annie
Modesitt

ROMANTIC
hand knits

For the Yarn Pirates.
Avast!

Annie Modesitt

ROMANTIC
hand knits

26 Flirtatious Designs
That Flatter Your Figure

Photography by
Thayer Allyson Gowdy

POTTER
CRAFT

New York

Published in the United States by Potter Craft,
an imprint of the Crown Publishing Group,
a division of Random House, Inc., New York.
www.crownpublishing.com
www.pottercraft.com

POTTER CRAFT & Colophon and POTTER & colophon
are registered trademarks of Random House, Inc.

Library of Congress Cataloging-in-Publication Data
Modesitt, Annie.
    Romantic hand knits : 26 flirtatious designs that flatter your figure /
by Annie Modesitt. — 1st ed.
        p. cm.
    Includes bibliographical references and index.
    ISBN 978-0-307-34696-4 (hardcover : alk. paper)
1. Knitting–Patterns.   2. Women's clothing.   I. Title.
    TT825.M624 2007
    746.43'2041–dc22   2006038507

ISBN: 978-0-307-34696-4

Printed in China

Cover and graphic design by Amy Sly

The publisher wishes to thank stylist Karen Schaupeter,
as well as Albright Inc, Astrid Schumacher, Bijoutique,
Buqet, Desideri Design, Mia Kim Design, Nature vs. Future,
Robin Page, Selma Karaca, Sohung Designs, The Point NYC,
Three Turtle Doves, and Volition for their gererous lending of props.

10 9 8 7 6 5 4 3 2 1

First Edition

Contents

Above the Waist

Below the Waist

Accessories

Resources

What Exactly Is Romance?

Is romance all about sexy lingerie and boudoir photos? Breathless good-byes on train platforms and weeks at sea exploring new lands? Or is romance more accessible than many of us imagine?

I've never been what I would call a *romantic* type. I'm pragmatic, a Virgo, and of Dutch ancestry in the bargain, so I'm generally the one to call if you need your books arranged in subject/author order or your front stoop swept and scrubbed. *Romantic*, though, is not a word that many of my friends would choose to describe me.

When I was younger, I thought I was too *smart* to be romantic. Romantics were a trifle dim, weren't they? As I grew older, I thought I was too busy to be romantic. Who had time for all those rose petals and diaphanous drapery? I had friends—I dated (occasionally)—but I didn't see myself as *romantic*. Perhaps I was afraid of seeming absurd; romance is for beautiful people, right?

While performing in a community theater production of *Baby*, a musical about several couples and their experiences with parenting, I heard one of the characters sing the line:

"Romance, romance—the one thing without which life isn't worth living . . ."

and I considered for the first time that romance might *not* be out of reach for an average, pragmatic, slightly zaftig woman like me.

Could it be that romance is integral to a well-rounded life? Is it possible that it isn't about being beautiful, or thin, or young, or rich—or even about love or sex?

Romance, it finally dawned on me, is about *dreams*. It's an idealized vision of something and our attempts to attain it. Romance is *wish fulfillment*, a belief that a certain type of perfection is possible within our imperfect lives. Romance is *hope*, surrendering ourselves to the quest for that perfection.

I began to explore the idea of romance, not just from the perspective of falling-in-love-with-another-person, but more as a matter of falling-in-love-with-*life*. Romance became a lens through which I could view life—not perfect, but idealized. I fell in love with the idea of romance! Beautiful clothing, exquisite dinners, exciting destinations—and the quest for the perfect yarn—all took on an unashamed, romantic aspect.

In knitting, as in romance, much of the joy is in the dream. I've always loved romantic films. When I was in my 20s, I spent many weekends at the revival film houses in New York enjoying witty dialogue, clever plot twists, and beautiful stars. The pieces in this book have been named in homage to my favorite films; perhaps you'll slip one into the DVD player as you knit it up. Planning these projects, swooning over the texture of a swatch, delighting in an interesting stitch pattern that creates a flattering illusion—these aspects of creating this book have afforded me more fun than any designer should be allowed to have! Not every design will look wonderful on every knitter—heaven knows many wouldn't be advisable for me—but I tried to provide a variety of silhouettes and styles with the hope that you will fall in love with something within these pages.

So as you leaf through these designs, wondering—as we all do—which might look best on you, know that you don't have to be perfect to create a beautiful and romantic look. Romance is not about perfection!

Above the Waist

The garment that dresses the top of the body sets the tone for the rest of your ensemble—a collar frames your face, sleeves and cuffs act as background for expressive hands, and the bust area is the most important fit point on any woman's body. Too often we simply toss on a T-shirt for comfort, when a beautiful handknit sweater could be just as easy to wear, and much more stunning.

Lacework, the drape of a fabric, stretchy ribbing, and a bit of strategic shaping are utilized here to lend an air of romantic illusion to the modest handknit sweater. With feminine details that flatter, worked in sumptuous yarns, these sweaters will become the garments you slip on for that special evening or to make any evening memorable.

A variety of silhouettes are presented for your perusal, perfect for day or evening wear, business or casual occasions. Enjoy these tops, which are certain to bring out the romantic in you.

Saratoga

So who says a decent backhand isn't sexy? This easy-to-knit banded tank top is based on a 1920s bathing suit, with interesting shaping around the armholes and neckline and matching striped trim at the hem. Make this as long or as short as you like—it's your serve!

Skill Level
EASY

SIZES

To fit bust: 28 (32, 36, 40, 44, 50)" (71 [82, 91, 101.5, 112, 127] cm)

FINISHED MEASUREMENTS

Bust: 28¾ (32, 36¾, 40, 44¾, 51¼)" (73 [82, 93.4, 101.5, 113.7, 130.2] cm)

Length: 24 (24½, 25, 26, 27, 27½)" (61.5 [62.2, 63.5, 66, 68.5, 70] cm)

MATERIALS

Star by Classic Elite (1¾ oz [50 g] skeins, each approx 112 yds [102 m], 99% cotton, 1% lycra)

A: Gold Dust 5160, 5 (5, 6, 6, 6, 7) skeins or 527 (573, 618, 670, 720, 786) yds (480.5 [522.5, 563.5, 611, 656.5, 717] m) of worsted weight yarn

B: Willow 5135, 1 (1, 1, 1, 1, 1) skein or 66 (72, 77, 84, 90, 98) yds (60 [65.5, 70, 76.5, 82, 89.5] m) of worsted weight yarn

C: Indian Paintbrush 5155, 1 (1, 1, 1, 1, 1) skein or 33 (36, 39, 42, 45, 49) yds (30 [33, 35.5, 38.5, 41, 44.5] m) of worsted weight yarn

D: Arizona Sun 5102, 1 (1, 1, 1, 1, 1) skein or 33 (36, 39, 42, 45, 49) yds (30 [33, 35.5, 38.5, 41, 44.5] m) of worsted weight yarn

Size 7 (4.5 mm) circular needle at least 24" (61 cm) long

Darning needle

Stitch holder

Stitch marker

Refer to glossary on page 136 for: Garter St, K2, P2 Rib, and PU&K.

GAUGE

20 sts and 28 rows = 4" (10 cm) in k2, p2 ribbing

BODY

Worked in the round.

With C, cast on 144 (160, 184, 200, 224, 256) sts.

Join and place marker to denote beg of round.

ROUNDS 1 AND 2: Work in garter st.

ROUNDS 3 AND 4: With B, work in garter st.

ROUNDS 5 AND 6: With D, work in garter st.

ROUNDS 7 AND 8: With A, work in garter st.

Rep Rounds 1–6 once more.

NEXT ROUND: With A, (k2, p2); rep to end of round.

Cont in k2, p2 ribbing as est until rib measures 15½ (15½, 16, 16½, 17, 17)" (39.5 [39.7, 41, 42.3, 43.6, 43.6] cm).

Divide sts evenly for Front and Back—72 (80, 92, 100, 112, 128) sts in each section. Place Front sts aside to work later.

BACK

Worked back and forth.

Detail of neck edging.

ARMHOLE

Continue in k2, p2 ribbing and working back and forth on Back sts only, BO 2 (2, 3, 2, 2, 4) sts at beg of next 2 rows, then BO 2 (2, 2, 3, 3, 3) sts at each Armhole edge 6 times—40 (48, 56, 56, 68, 76) sts rem.

Work even until Armhole measures 8½ (9, 9, 9½, 10, 10½)" (21.5 [23, 23, 24, 25.5, 26.5] cm).

GARTER STITCH NECK EDGING

ROWS 1 AND 2: Work in garter st.

ROWS 3 AND 4: With B, work in garter st.

ROWS 5 AND 6: With D, work in garter st.

ROWS 7 AND 8: With A, work in garter st.

Repeat Rows 1–2 once more for a total of 10 rows.

BO all sts loosely with C.

FRONT

Worked back and forth.

ARMHOLE

Work Armhole shaping as for Back, then work even until Front measures 4 (4, 3½, 3½, 3½, 3½)" (10 [10, 9, 9, 9, 9] cm).

Work garter stitch neck edging as for Back, BO all sts loosely with C.

SHOULDERS AND ARMHOLE BANDS

Worked in the round.

With C and right side facing, start at upper left corner of Back and PU&K 36 (37, 36, 37, 39, 40) sts down left Back Armhole plus 23 (23, 20, 20, 20, 20) sts up left Front Armhole. Cable cast on 23 (25, 28, 30, 33, 35)

sts—82 (85, 84, 87, 92, 95) sts. Join to knit in the round.

Work garter stitch stripes with decreases as follows:

ROUND 1: With C, knit, dec 5 sts around all sts—77 (80, 79, 82, 87, 90) sts.

ROUND 2 AND ALL EVEN-NUMBERED ROUNDS: Purl in the same color as the previous round.

ROUND 3: With B, knit, dec 5 sts around all sts—72 (75, 74, 77, 82, 85) sts.

ROUND 5: With D, knit, dec 5 sts around all sts—67 (70, 69, 72, 77, 80) sts.

ROUND 7: With A, knit, dec 5 sts around all sts—62 (65, 64, 67, 72, 75) sts.

ROUND 9: With C, knit, dec 5 sts around all sts—57 (60, 59, 62, 67, 70) sts.

ROUND 10: With C, purl.

Rep Rounds 3–10 with no further decreasing.

BO all sts loosely.

Repeat on second Armhole.

FINISHING

Steam-block, weave in ends.

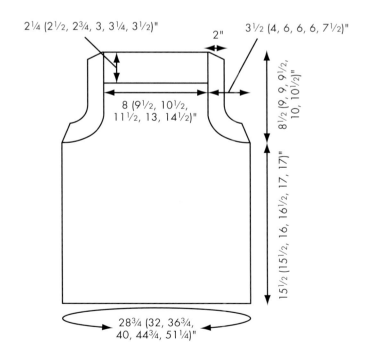

2¼ (2½, 2¾, 3, 3¼, 3½)"

2"

3½ (4, 6, 6, 6, 7½)"

8 (9½, 10½, 11½, 13, 14½)"

8½ (9, 9, 9½, 10, 10½)"

15½ (15½, 16, 16½, 17, 17)"

28¾ (32, 36¾, 40, 44¾, 51¼)"

Ninotchka

So what's a girl to do who's—ahem—relatively well endowed when all of those thin little spaghetti strap tank tops are floating around? Make one with a shelf bra inside, that's what! Short-row shaping and a very elastic yarn for the bra, combined with a wide band of sewn-in elastic at the bottom of the bra, will give you the beauty and support that you deserve with this shelf-bra silk tank!

Skill Level
INTERMEDIATE

SIZES
To fit bust: 28 (32, 36, 40, 44, 48)" (71.8 [82.1, 92.3, 102.6, 112.8, 123.1] cm)

FINISHED MEASUREMENTS
Bust: 30 (34, 38, 42, 46, 50)" (76.9 [87.2, 97.4, 107.7, 117.9, 128.2] cm)

Length: 16 (17, 18, 19, 20, 21)" (41 [43.6, 46.2, 48.7, 51.3, 53.8] cm)

MATERIALS
A: Silk Rhapsody by Artyarns (3½ oz [100 g] skeins, each approx 260 yds [238 m], 100% silk with 70% mohair, 30% silk), Raspberry Pink RH245, 2 (3, 3, 3, 3, 3) skeins or 589 (653, 717, 781, 845, 909) yds (537 [595.5, 654, 712.5, 770.5, 829] m) of worsted weight yarn

B: Fixation by Cascade (1¾ oz [50 g] balls, each approx 100 yds [92 m], 98.3% cotton, 1.7% elastic), Red 7219, 1 (2, 2, 2, 2, 2) balls or 139 (155, 171, 185, 202, 215) yds (127 [141.5, 155, 168.5, 182.5, 196] m) of sportweight yarn

C: Regal Silk 101 by Artyarns (1¾ oz [50 g] skeins, each approx 163 yds [149m], 100% silk), Raspberry Pink RS245, 1 (1, 1, 2, 2, 2) balls or 199 (222, 242, 263, 285, 307) yds (181.5 [200.5, 220.5, 242, 262, 280] m) of sportweight yarn

D: Silk Mohair by Artyarns (88 oz [25 g] skeins, each approx 230 yds [210 m], Pinks MS413, 1 (1, 1, 2, 2, 2) balls or 280 (311, 341, 372, 402, 432) yds (255.5 [283.5, 311, 339.5, 366.5, 394] m) of laceweight yarn

E: Silk Rhapsody by Artyarns, Browns RH113, 1 (1, 1, 1, 1, 1) skein or 91 (101, 112, 131, 140, 150) yds (83 [91, 100.5, 109.5, 118.5, 127.5] m) of worsted weight yarn

Size 4 (3.5 mm) circular needle 24" (61 cm) long

Size 5 (3.75 mm) circular needle 24" (61 cm) long

Size 8 (5 mm) circular needle 24" (61 cm) long

Stitch markers

Darning needle

Elastic, ⅜" (9 mm) wide, cut to rib cage measurement plus 2" (5 cm)

Sewing needle and thread

Refer to glossary on page 136 for: 3-needle BO, I-Cord BO, K2togR, K2, P2 Rib, M1, Provisional Cast-On, PU&K, St st, Twisted Cord, VDD, W&T, and YO.

GAUGE
6 sts and 8 rows = 1" (2.5 cm) in stockinette stitch using medium needle

BODICE
Using a provisional cast-on, with medium needle and A, cast on 180 (204, 228, 252, 276, 300) sts.

Knit 2 rows. Join, placing marker to note start of round.

Shelf-Bra inside-out detail.

EYELET ROUND: (K2togR, YO, k2); rep around all sts.

NEXT ROUND: Purl.

NEXT ROUND: Knit.

Cont in St st until piece measures 7 (7½, 8, 8½, 9, 9½)" (18 [19.2, 20.5, 21.8, 23.1, 24.4] cm) from cast-on. Do not bind off, set sts aside.

SHELF BRA

With smallest needles and B, cast on 168 (192, 216, 240, 264, 288) sts.

Work back and forth in St st for ½" (1.25 cm), ending with a RS row.

NEXT ROW (WS): Knit, join sts, and place marker to note start of round (this will mark the left side of the body).

NEXT ROUND (RS): (K2, p2); rep around all sts.

Cont in k2, p2 ribbing as est for 1" (2.5 cm).

NEXT ROUND: K15 (17, 19, 21, 23, 25) m1; repeat 6 times more for front, place second marker at side seam, knit to end of round (back)—180 (204, 228, 252, 276, 300) sts.

NEXT ROUND (FRONT SHORT-ROW SHAPING): K to 2 sts before second marker, W&T, work back to 2 sts before first marker, W&T.

NEXT ROUND: Knit all sts.

Rep last 2 rounds until piece measures 5⅛ (5⅛, 6⅛, 5¼, 6¼, 7¾)" (13.1 [13.1, 15.7, 13.5, 16, 19.9] cm) from start of rib when measured across non-short-row (back) area.

Note: For larger cup sizes, you may want to work the entire front short-row shaping again in part or in its entirety.

JOINING BRA TO BODICE

Place pieces with right sides together and wrong sides facing out.

With medium needle and E, join pieces with 3-needle BO. Turn joined piece inside out so that bra is to the inside and St st of Bodice is facing out. Steam-block join gently.

TOP EDGE TRIM

With medium needle and E, PU&K 180 (204, 228, 252, 276, 300) sts around top of work at join, k1 round, then BO all sts using I-cord BO.

PEPLUM

Slip provisional sts onto circ needle, place marker to note center back.

NEXT ROUND: With largest needle and C, *k15 (17, 19, 21, 23, 25) sts, m1; rep from * 12 times around all sts—192 (216, 240, 264, 288, 312) sts.

NEXT ROUND: Knit all sts.

NEXT 10 ROUNDS: Work Rows 1 and 2 of Lace Chart 3 times, then change to D and work Rows 3 and 4 of Lace Chart twice.

Repeat these 10 rounds until piece measures approx 8 (8½, 9, 9½, 10, 10½)" (20.5 [21.5, 23, 24, 25.4, 26.7] cm), then change to E and work Rows 1 and 2 of Lace Chart 3 more times.

Knit 1 round, purl 1 round.

BO all sts loosely.

FINISHING

Steam-block piece through outer layer and bra.

With B and a darning needle, turn bottom (St st section) of bra up and sew in place, creating a casing. Slip the elastic into the casing through the nonjoined edge sts from first rows of bra. Tack ends of elastic together using sewing needle and thread.

Try on top to determine length of shoulder ties from top edge of tank to top of shoulder. With E, make 2 Twisted Cord ties that measure twice this length. Tack in place on front and back of bodice.

With E, make a twisted cord to measure around rib cage plus 8" (20.5 cm). Draw this cord through eyelets at top of lace section, and arrange cord so the ties hang down in the center front.

With E, make a 10" (25.4 cm) piece of I-cord and tie it into a bow. Tack this to the I-cord BO at the center front of the tank.

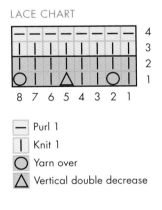

LACE CHART

4 — — — — — — — —
3 | | | | | | | |
2 | | | | | | | |
1 O | | △ | | O |

8 7 6 5 4 3 2 1

— Purl 1
| Knit 1
O Yarn over
△ Vertical double decrease

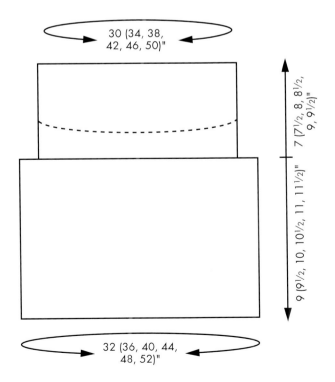

30 (34, 38, 42, 46, 50)"

7 (7½, 8, 8½, 9, 9½)"

9 (9½, 10, 10½, 11, 11½)"

32 (36, 40, 44, 48, 52)"

Adam's Rib

Tailored garments have their own romantic appeal. Aside from flattering just about any figure type, they provide a perfect canvas for pearls, silk scarves, brooches, belts—any type of accessory you can imagine. This Chesterfield jacket is worked in five pieces (fronts, back, sleeves), then decorative chain embroidery trim is worked to create faux princess seams before assembling.

Skill Level
INTERMEDIATE

SIZE
To fit bust: 32 (34, 38, 42, 46, 49)" (81 [86, 96.6, 106.5, 117, 124.5] cm)

FINISHED MEASUREMENTS
Bust: 37 (41, 45, 50, 54, 58)" (94 [104, 114, 127, 137, 147] cm)

Length: 22¾ (24, 24½, 25¾, 27, 27¾)" (58 [61, 62.5, 65.5, 68.5, 70.5] cm)

MATERIALS
A: Grace by Lorna's Laces (2 oz [57 g] skeins, each approx 120 yds [109 m], mohair blend), Black Pearl 27, 6 (6, 7, 7, 8, 8) skeins or 678 (731, 786, 825, 909, 953) yds (618.5 [666.5, 717, 752.5, 821, 869] m) loopy mohair bouclé yarn

B: Swirl DK by Lorna's Laces (2 oz [57 g] skeins, each approx 150 yds [137 m], 85% Merino wool, 15% silk), Manzanita 2NS, 4 (4, 5, 5, 5, 6) skeins or 652 (704, 756, 794, 866, 917) yds (594.5 [642, 689.5, 724, 798, 836.5] m) sportweight yarn

C: Silk Chenille by Tilli Tomas (3½ oz [100 g] skeins, each approx 125 yds [114 m], 100% silk), Black, 1 (1, 1, 1, 2, 2) skeins or 136 (146, 157, 165, 181, 191) yds (124 [133, 143, 150.5, 164, 174] m) worsted weight yarn

Size 6 (4 mm) needles

Size 10 (6 mm) needles, or size to obtain gauge

8 red stitch markers, 2 blue stitch markers

Stitch holders

Darning needle

Size G/6 (4 mm) crochet hook

10 hooks and eyes

Refer to glossary on page 136 for: Sl st, VDD, W&T, and YO.

GAUGE
3.75 sts and 5 rows = 1" (2.5 cm) over stockinette stitch with one strand each of A and B held together using larger needle

BODY
With one strand each of A and B held together and using larger needles, cast on 140 (156, 172, 188, 204, 220) sts.

Switch to smaller needles and knit 3 rows, then purl 1 row.

SET UP DART-SHAPING SECTIONS
NEXT ROW (RS): Work and place markers as follows.

RIGHT FRONT
K1 (edge st), k11 (13, 15, 17, 19, 21), place red marker to note decrease point, k11 (11, 11, 11, 12,

12), place red marker (dart), k12 (14, 16, 18, 19, 21) sts, place blue marker to note right side of garment.

BACK

K12 (14, 16, 18, 19, 21) sts, place red marker, k11 (11, 11, 11, 12, 12), place red marker (dart), k12 (14, 16, 18, 20, 22) sts, place blue marker to note center back of garment, k12 (14, 16, 18, 20, 22) sts, place red marker, k11 (11, 11, 11, 12, 12), place red marker (dart), k12 (14, 16, 18, 19, 21) sts, place blue marker to note left side of garment.

LEFT FRONT

K12 (14, 16, 18, 19, 21) sts, place red marker, k11 (11, 11, 11, 12, 12) sts, place red marker (dart), k11 (13, 15, 17, 19, 21) sts, k1 (edge st).
NEXT ROW (WS): Purl all sts.

BEGIN GARTER/BASKET STITCH CHART

ROW 1 (RS): (K2, p2); rep to end of row, slipping markers.
ROW 2 (WS): Knit and purl stitches as they appear.
ROWS 3, 4, 7, AND 8: Knit.
ROW 5 (RS): (P2, k2); rep to end of row.
ROW 6 (WS): Knit and purl stitches as they appear.
Dec 1 st between each red marker set every RS row until no sts rem between red markers—96 (112, 128, 144, 156, 172 sts.
Note: When 1 st rem between markers, in next dec remove 1 marker, k2togR, then replace marker, creating a double marker.
Remove Back dart markers, but *do not remove* Front dart markers; they will sit as a double red marker through the next section of the jacket.
Cont working in pats as est on either side of red Front dart double markers until piece measures 5¾ (5¾, 6, 6, 6¼, 6¼)" (14.5 [14.5, 15, 15, 16, 16] cm) from start of Garter/Basket St Chart. End with a WS row.
NEXT ROW (RS): Work to first double red marker set (Right Front dart), m1 between markers. Work in pat as est to Left Front dart markers and m1 between markers as for Right Front—inc of 2 sts across row—98 (114, 130, 146, 158, 174) sts.

Note: No inc at back.
Inc in this manner between Front red marker sets every other row, working inc as St st until there are 128 (144, 160, 176, 192, 208) sts.
Cont working in pats as est on either side of red double markers with no further increases until piece measures 12¾ (12¾, 13½, 14, 14¾, 14¾)" (32.5 [32.5, 34.5, 35.5, 37.5, 37.5] cm) from start of Garter/Basket St Chart.

SEPARATE FOR BACK AND FRONTS

Slip Front sts (first and last 32 [36, 40, 44, 48, 52] sts) onto holders to work later.

ARMHOLE SHAPING

Working with 64 (72, 80, 88, 96, 104) Back sts only, BO 2 (2, 2, 2, 4, 4) sts at start of next 2 rows, then BO 2 (2, 2, 2, 2, 2) sts at start of next 4 rows—52 (60, 68, 76, 80, 88) sts rem.
Work even until Armhole measures 9¼ (10¼, 9¾, 10¼, 10¾, 11¼)" (23.7 [26.3, 25, 26.3, 27.6, 28.8] cm).

SHOULDER SHAPING

BO 5 (5, 7, 7, 8, 7) sts at beg of next 2 rows, then BO 6 (6, 6, 8, 7, 8) sts at beg of next 4 rows.
BO rem 18 (26, 30, 30, 36, 42) sts.

FRONTS

Return to Front sts—32 (36, 40, 44, 48, 52) sts in each Front. Working both sides at once, work armhole shaping as follows:
BO 2 (2, 2, 2, 4, 4) sts at Armhole edge once, then BO 2 (2, 2, 2, 2, 2) sts at Armhole edge twice—26 (30, 34, 38, 40, 44) sts rem for each front. Work even until Armhole depth measures 2½ (3¼, 2½, 2¾, 3, 3¼)" (6.4 [8.3, 6.4, 7, 7.6, 8.3] cm).

NECK SHAPING

At each Neck edge, working both Fronts together, BO 2 (3, 5, 4, 4, 4) sts once—24 (27, 29, 34, 36, 40) sts— then 1 (1, 1, 2, 2, 2) sts at Neck edge every row 4 times—20 (23, 25, 26, 28, 32) sts—then BO 1 (2, 2, 1,

2, 3) sts at Neck edge every other row 3 times—17 (17, 19, 23, 22, 23) sts rem each shoulder.

At the same time, when front armhole depth measures same as back, work to next shoulder edge and BO shoulder as follows.

SHOULDER SHAPING

BO 5 (5, 7, 7, 8, 7) sts at Shoulder edge every other row once, then BO 6 (6, 6, 8, 7, 8) sts at Shoulder edge every other row twice.

SLEEVES (MAKE 2)

With C and using larger needles, cast on 28 (32, 32, 32, 36, 40) sts.

Switch to smaller needles and work 10 rows in garter st, then work 4 rows in St st, ending with a WS row.

NEXT ROW (RS): With one strand each of A and B held together, knit 1 row.

Beg Garter/Basket St Chart used in body, and beg inc 1 st each edge every 4 (2, 4, 4, 4, 4) rows 19 (21, 19, 21, 20, 20) times—66 (74, 70, 74, 76, 80) sts.

Work even until Sleeve measures 18¾ (19, 20, 21, 23¼, 25½)" (47.5 [48.5, 51, 53.5, 59, 64.8] cm) from cast-on. End with a WS row.

CAP SHAPING

BO 8 (9, 10, 9, 9, 9) sts at beg of next 2 rows, then BO 3 (3, 3, 3, 3, 3) sts at beg next 4 rows, then BO 1 (2, 2, 4, 3, 3) sts at beg next 2 rows—36 (40, 34, 36, 40, 44) sts.

Work even with no shaping for 0 (0, 2, 6, 6, 6) rows, then BO 3 (3, 3, 4, 5, 4) sts at start of next 2 rows 4 (4, 3, 2, 2, 3) times, BO rem 12 (16, 16, 20, 20, 20) sts.

FINISHING

Steam-block all pieces.

PLACKETS

With RS facing and a single strand of C, using smaller needles PU&K 70 (72, 74, 70, 80, 82) sts along Left Front edge.

Work in garter st for 8 rows, BO all sts loosely.
Rep for Right Front.

NECKBAND

With RS facing and a strand of C, using smaller needles, PU&K 96 (96, 102, 102, 102, 108) sts around neck opening, including top of plackets.

NEXT ROW (WS): Knit all sts.
NEXT ROW (RS): K28 (28, 30, 30, 30, 32) sts, W&T.
NEXT ROW (WS): Knit back to center Front opening.
NEXT ROW (RS): Knit to 2 sts before last W&T, W&T.
Rep last 2 rows until 8 sts rem to be worked at center Front, end with a WS row.
NEXT ROW (RS): Knit all sts, slipping wrap from each W&T onto left needle and working it along with wrapped st.
NEXT ROW (WS): K28 (28, 30, 30, 30, 32) sts, W&T.
NEXT ROW (RS): Knit back to center Front opening.
NEXT ROW (WS): Knit to 2 sts before last W&T, W&T.

Rep last 2 rows until 8 sts rem to be worked at center Front, end with a WS row.

NEXT ROW (WS): Knit all sts, slipping wrap from each W&T onto left needle and working it along with wrapped st. Work in garter st for 2 rows.

NEXT ROW (WS): (K2, k2togR, k2); rep to end—80 (80, 85, 85, 85, 90) sts rem.

Work 3 more rows in garter st, then BO all sts loosely. Sew Shoulder seams and underarm seams. Turn jacket and Sleeve inside out and stitch Sleeve into Armhole.

CLOSURES

Measure along WS of left placket and Front neckband and space 10 hooks evenly along edge so that hook sits 1/16" (2 mm) from edge of jacket. Sew hooks in place. Match eyes to hooks and sew to wrong side of right Placket and Neckband so that edge of eye sits 1/16" (2 mm) in from edge of jacket. Sew eyes in place. Sew Shoulder seams and underarm seams. Turn jacket and Sleeves inside out and stitch Sleeves into Armhole.

GARTER/BASKET ST CHART

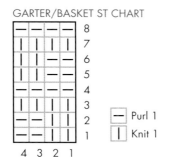

— Purl 1
| Knit 1

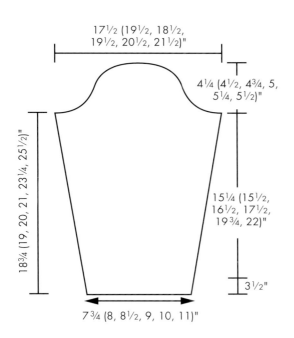

17½ (19½, 18½, 19½, 20½, 21½)"

4¼ (4½, 4¾, 5, 5¼, 5½)"

18¾ (19, 20, 21, 23¼, 25½)"

15¼ (15½, 16½, 17½, 19¾, 22)"

3½"

7¾ (8, 8½, 9, 10, 11)"

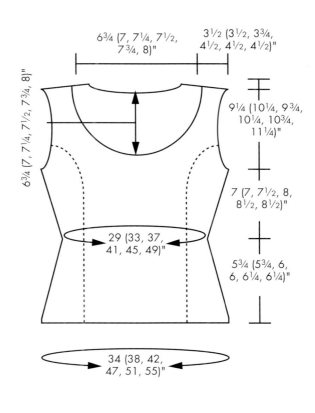

6¾ (7, 7¼, 7½, 7¾, 8)"

3½ (3½, 3¾, 4½, 4½, 4½)"

6¾ (7, 7¼, 7½, 7¾, 8)"

9¼ (10¼, 9¾, 10¼, 10¾, 11¼)"

7 (7, 7½, 8, 8½, 8½)"

29 (33, 37, 41, 45, 49)"

5¾ (5¾, 6, 6, 6¼, 6¼)"

34 (38, 42, 47, 51, 55)"

The Heiress

The period is Edwardian; the details, sublime. This sweet embroidered cardigan is actually a very simple pattern with a touch of lace at the hem, cuff, and neckline. Embroidered flowers are added after the cardigan is finished. A provisional cast-on is used for the hem and cuffs of this sweater.

Skill Level
INTERMEDIATE

SIZE
To fit bust: 29 (35, 40, 44, 50, 56)" (74 [89, 101.5, 112, 127, 142] cm)

FINISHED MEASUREMENTS
Bust: 28½ (33¾, 41, 46¼, 53¼, 58¾)" (72.5 [85.8, 104, 117.5, 135.3, 147] cm)

Length: 31 (32, 32½, 33½, 34, 35½)" (79 [81, 82.5, 85, 86, 90] cm)

MATERIALS
A: Ksar by Bouton d'Or (1¾ oz [50 g] skeins, each approx 91 yds [83 m], 50% camel, 50% wool), Veloute Blue 612, 8 (9, 11, 11, 12, 13) skeins or 750 (838, 919, 1006, 1094, 1182) yds (684 [764.5, 838, 917.5, 997.5, 1078] m) of worsted weight yarn

B: Ksar by Bouton d'Or, Flamant Rose 632, 2 (2, 3, 3, 3, 3) skeins or 188 (209, 232, 252, 274, 296) yds (171.5 [190.5, 212, 232, 252, 270] m) of worsted weight yarn

C: Victoria by Anny Blatt (1¾ oz [50 g] skeins, each approx 109 yds [99 m], 100% nylon), Ruben Red, 1 (1, 1, 1, 1, 1) ball or 82 (92, 101, 111, 121, 130) yds (75 [84, 92, 100.5, 109.5, 118.5] m) sportweight ribbon yarn

D: Victoria by Anny Blatt, Gold, 1 (1, 1, 1, 1, 1) ball or 62 (69, 76, 83, 99, 107) yds (56.5 [63, 69.5, 75.5, 82, 88.5] m) sportweight ribbon yarn

E: Victoria by Anny Blatt, Calista Green, 1 (1, 1, 1, 1, 1) ball or 62 (69, 76, 83, 99, 107) yds (56.5 [63, 69.5, 75.5, 82, 88.5] m) sportweight ribbon yarn

Size 6 (4 mm) circular needle 36" (91 cm) long for facings

Size 8 (5 mm) circular needle 36" (91 cm) long, or size to obtain gauge

Size 10 (6 mm) circular needle 36" (91 cm) long

See Circular Stress, page 112, for thoughts on circular needle lengths.

Darning needle

Seven ½" (1.25 cm) buttons

Refer to glossary on page 136 for: Garter St, I-Bobble, K2togL, K2togR, Provisional Cast-On, VDD, K2tog Picot BO, and YO. See page 29 for embroidery stitches: Decorative Chain Embroidery, French Knot, Satin Stitch.

GAUGE
4.5 and 5 rows = 1" (2.5 cm) over Rib Chart Pattern using medium needle and A

BODY
Using a provisional cast-on, with A and medium needle, CO 128 (152, 184, 208, 240, 264) sts.

NEXT ROW (RS): Starting with st 2 (2, 1, 3, 2, 2), work Row 1 of Rib Chart across all sts, end with st 5 (5, 6, 4, 5, 5). Work in rib pat as est until piece measures 21¾ (22¼, 22¾, 23¼, 23¾, 24¼)" (55.3 [56.5, 58, 59, 60, 61.5] cm). End with a WS row.

NEXT ROW (RS): Work in pat across 32 (38, 46, 52, 60, 66) sts, place these sts on holder for Right Front. Cont working in pat across next 64 (76, 92, 104, 120, 132) sts for Back. Place rem 32 (38, 46, 52, 60, 66) sts on holder for Left Front.

The Heiress lace edging and embroidery.

row twice—13 (16, 22, 25, 30, 34) sts rem in each shoulder.

At the same time, when Armhole depth measures same as Back, work Shoulder shaping as follows:
BO 5 (6, 8, 9, 10, 12) sts at shoulder edge once, then BO 4 (5, 7, 8, 10, 11) sts at shoulder edge twice.

SLEEVES (MAKE 2)

Using a provisional cast-on, with A and medium needle, CO 36 (36, 36, 42, 42, 48) sts.

NEXT ROW (RS): Work Row 1 of Rib Chart across all sts.

Continue in pat, and *at the same time,* inc 1 st each edge every 4 rows 17 (20, 20, 18, 21, 20) times—70 (76, 76, 78, 84, 88) sts.

Continue in rib pat as est until piece measures 14½ (15½, 16½, 17½, 18½, 19½)" (37 [39.5, 42, 44.5, 47, 49.5] cm). End with a WS row.

CAP SHAPING

BO 8 (8, 8, 8, 10, 10) sts at beg of next 2 rows, then BO 2 (2, 4, 4, 4, 4) sts at beg next 4 rows, then BO 5 (5, 5, 3, 3, 3) sts at beg next 4 rows, work even with no shaping for 8 (8, 10, 10, 10, 12) rows, then BO 6 (4, 4, 3, 4, 5) sts at start of next 2 rows 1 (2, 1, 2, 2, 2) times. BO rem 14 (16, 16, 22, 20, 20) sts.

FINISHING

Steam-block all pieces. Sew Shoulder seams and fit Sleeves into armholes, basting them first for a good fit. Sew underarm and side seams.

PLACKET

Starting at left Front Neck edge, PU&K 120 (120, 120, 126, 132, 132) sts down left Front.

NEXT ROW (WS): Knit.

NEXT ROW (RS): Knit.

Cont in garter st until 8 rows of left Placket have been worked. End with a RS row. BO all sts.

Starting at right Front bottom edge, PU&K 120 (120, 120, 126, 132, 132) sts up right Front.

NEXT 3 ROWS: Knit.

NEXT ROW: K8 (8, 8, 9, 9, 9) sts, (BO 3 sts, k17 [17, 17, 18, 19, 19] sts) 5 times, BO 3, k9 (9, 9, 9, 10, 10) sts.

BACK ARMHOLE SHAPING

Working with Back sts only, BO 4 (4, 6, 6, 8, 10) sts at beg of next 2 rows, then BO 3 (3, 4, 4, 5, 5) sts at each Armhole edge twice—44 (52, 64, 72, 84, 92) sts rem. Work even until Armhole depth measures 8¼ (8¾, 8¾, 9¼, 9¾, 10¼)" (21.5 [22, 22, 23.5, 24.5, 26] cm).

SHOULDER SHAPING

BO 5 (6, 8, 9, 10, 12) sts at beg of next 2 rows, then BO 4 (5, 7, 8, 10, 11) sts at beg of next 4 rows—18 (24, 20, 26, 24, 24) sts rem at center Back.
Place Back sts on holder.

FRONT ARMHOLE SHAPING

Working both Fronts together, BO 4 (4, 6, 6, 8, 10) sts at Armhole edge twice, then BO 3 (4, 5, 4, 5, 5) sts at Armhole edge twice—22 (26, 32, 36, 42, 46) sts rem in each Front.

Continue rib pat until Front Armhole measures 5⅜ (5⅞, 5¾, 7, 6⅝, 7)" (13.5 [15, 14.5, 18, 17, 18] cm).

NECK SHAPING

Working both Fronts *at the same time,* at each Neck edge BO 5 (6, 6, 7, 8, 8) sts once, then BO 1 st at Neck edge every row twice, then BO 1 st at Neck edge every other row twice, then BO 1 st at Neck edge every fourth

NEXT ROW: Knit, casting on 3 sts over each BO section. Cont in garter st until 8 rows of right Placket have been worked. End with a RS row. BO all sts.

LACE EDGINGS

CUFF

Transfer 36 (36, 36, 42, 42, 48) provisionally cast-on sts at Cuff to medium needle. With B, purl 1 round, place marker at start of round.

NEXT ROUND: Inc 6 (inc 6, inc 6, inc 0, inc 0, dec 6) sts evenly around all sts—42 sts.

Work Row 1 of Lace Chart around all sts 3 times, placing a marker between each pat rep and omitting st 15 (yellow st).

Cont in charted pat as est, working to Row 20 of chart. BO all sts using k2tog picot BO.

HEM

Transfer 128 (152, 184, 208, 240, 264) provisionally cast-on sts at Hem to larger circ needle, then with RS facing and B, PU&K 4 sts at bottom of each Placket—136 (160, 192, 216, 248, 272) sts.

NEXT ROW (RS): Knit.

NEXT ROW (WS): Inc 5 (9, 5, 9, 5, 9) sts evenly across—141 (169, 197, 225, 253, 281) sts.

Work sts 1–14 of Row 1 of Lace Chart across all sts 10 (12, 14, 16, 18, 20) times, ending with st 15 (yellow st) in chart, placing a marker between each pat rep.

Cont in charted pat as est, working to Row 20 of chart and working edge st in garter st (knit the first and last st of every row).

BO all sts using k2tog picot BO.

COLLAR

With WS facing (so that PU seam will lay under the collar when it folds over), use B and size 8 circs to PU&K 71 (71, 71, 71, 85, 99) sts around Neck edge.

Work 3 rows in garter st, change to largest needle.

Work Row 1 of Lace Chart across all sts 5 (5, 5, 5, 6, 7) times, ending with st 15 (yellow st) in chart. Place a marker between each pat rep.

Cont in charted pat as est, working to Row 20 of chart and working edge st in each row in garter st (knit each row).

BO all sts using k2tog picot BO.
Weave in ends.

EMBROIDERY

Work charted ribbon embroidery randomly across Hem, Sleeves, and body of sweater, using embroidery chart as a guide in the following manner: With E and crochet hook, work decorative chain embroidery along Fronts and around Hem, following embroidery chart but also working free-form and loosely. (Have fun; if you don't like what you've done, it's very easy to pull out!)

When chain st "vines" have been worked around the sweater, use C and a darning needle to work French knots and satin st embroidery using embroidery chart as a guide. Repeat with D. Weave in ends.

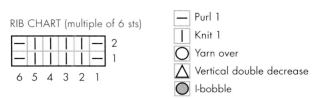

RIB CHART (multiple of 6 sts)

— Purl 1

| Knit 1

O Yarn over

△ Vertical double decrease

◉ I-bobble

LACE CHART (multiple of 14 sts + 1)

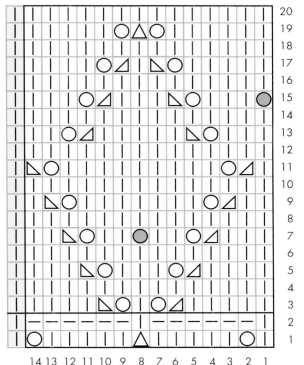

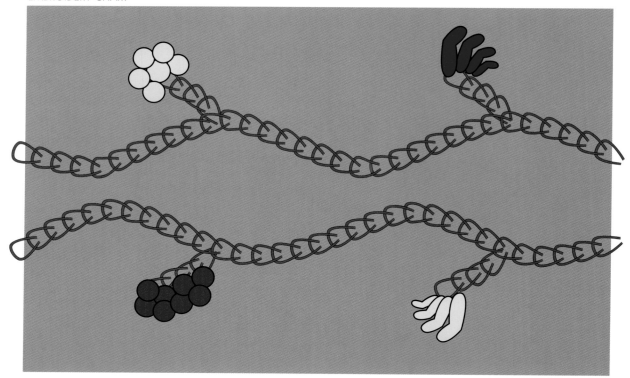

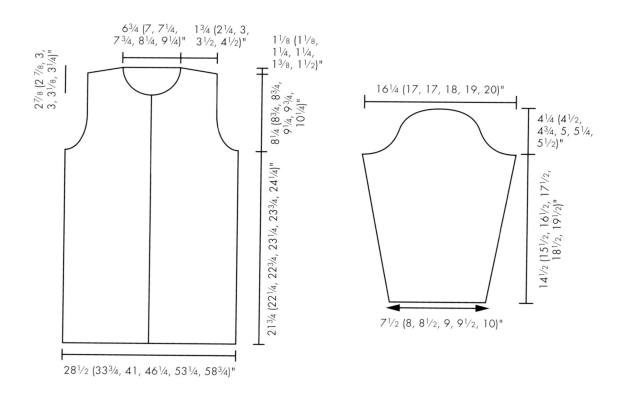

6¾ (7, 7¼, 7¾, 8¼, 9¼)"

1¾ (2¼, 3, 3½, 4½)"

1⅛ (1⅛, 1¼, 1¼, 1⅜, 1½)"

2⅞ (2⅞, 3, 3, 3⅛, 3¼)"

8¼ (8¾, 8¾, 9¼, 9¾, 10¼)"

21¾ (22¼, 22¾, 23¼, 23¾, 24¼)"

28½ (33¾, 41, 46¼, 53¼, 58¾)"

16¼ (17, 17, 18, 19, 20)"

4¼ (4½, 4¾, 5, 5¼, 5½)"

14½ (15½, 16½, 17½, 18½, 19½)"

7½ (8, 8½, 9, 9½, 10)"

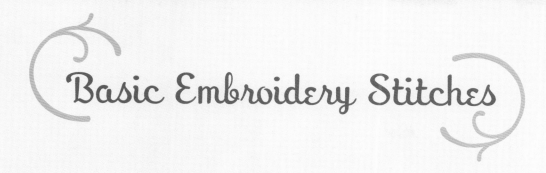

Basic Embroidery Stitches

DECORATIVE CHAIN EMBROIDERY

Holding the yarn at the back of the work, insert the hook from the front to the back. Yarn over, draw loop through to the front of the fabric. (Move hook to point where next chain should start and insert from the front to the back. Yarn over, draw loop through fabric and through loop on hook.) Repeat, moving the hook at the start of each new stitch to create a decorative pattern on the front of the fabric. Continue in this way, following the design line.

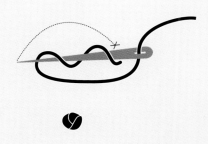

FRENCH KNOT

Bring the thread out from the back to the front of the work and hold down with thumb or finger. Working close to the fabric, wrap the yarn loosely several times around needle (generally 4 to 6 wraps). Using the section of the yarn nearest the eye of the needle, wrap once more near the point of the needle (this will lock the knot in place).

Insert the needle into the point where you would like the knot (*not* at the exact same point where the yarn emerges or it will simply pull back through).

Pull the needle through to the back, leaving a small knot on the surface and holding your finger over the knot until all yarn is completely pulled to the back.

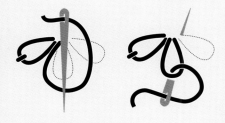

LOOP PETAL

Pull the yarn to the front of the work, then reinsert the needle into the same place and, in the same motion, slip it out again at the point where you'd like the edge of the flower petal to be, catching the loop with the needle on the right side of the work. Tighten until loop draws closed, then reinsert needle a half-stitch away from designated petal edge.

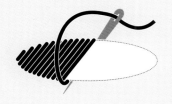

SATIN STITCH

Work straight stitches closely together across the designated shape, keeping edges even.

A Streetcar Named Desire

Blanche DuBois may have depended on the kindness of strangers a little too much, but the woman certainly knew how to dress! This kimono (in the Southern sense of the word) styled pink tulip cardigan is worked in Bamboo yarn for a drape that is absolutely astounding. Shirring at the shoulders and an I-cord belt add to the boudoir feeling. *Honey, would you run get me a lemon Coke, with plenty of chipped ice?*

Skill Level
INTERMEDIATE

SIZE
To fit bust: 28 (32, 36, 40, 44, 50)" (71 [82, 91, 101.5, 112, 127] cm)

FINISHED MEASUREMENTS
Bust: 30¼ (37¾, 37¾, 45¼, 45¼, 52¾)" (77 [96, 96, 115, 115, 134] cm)

Length: 22¾ (23½, 24¼, 25½, 26, 26¾)" (58 [59.5, 61.5, 65, 66, 68] cm)

MATERIALS
Royal Bamboo by Plymouth Yarns (1¾ oz [50g] skeins, each approx 93 yds [85 m] 100% Bamboo), Pink 04, 11 skeins or 722 (783, 846, 917, 976, 1063) yds (658 [714, 771, 836, 899, 970] m) worsted weight yarn

Size 6 (4 mm) circular needle at least 24" (61 cm) long

Size 7 (4.5 mm) circular needle at least 24" (61 cm) long, or size to obtain gauge

Darning needle

Stitch holders

Stitch markers

GAUGE
4.5 sts and 6 rows = 1" (2.5 cm) over Chart B using larger needle

Refer to glossary on page 136 for: I-Bobble, VDD, and YO.

BODY
With smaller needle, CO 137 (171, 171, 205, 205, 239) sts.

Knit 2 rows.

Work Rows 1–6 of Chart A once.

Work Rows 1–4 of Chart C once, dec 1 st on last row of chart—136 (170, 170, 204, 204, 238) sts.

NEXT ROW (RS): Change to larger needles and work Chart B across all sts, placing a marker after each repeat. Work Chart B as est to Row 24, then work 4 rows of Chart C.

NEXT ROW (RS): Work Chart D across all sts, placing a marker after each repeat.

Continue working Chart D until piece measures 12¾ (12¾, 13½, 14, 14¾, 14¾)" (32.5 [32.5, 34.5, 35.5, 37.5, 37.5] cm) from eyelet row—Row 3 of Chart A.

DIVIDE FRONTS AND BACK
NEXT ROW (RS): Cont in Chart D as est, work 34 (42, 42, 51, 51, 59) right Front sts, put these sts on holder. Work across 68 (86, 86, 102, 102, 120) Back sts. Put rem 34 (42, 42, 51, 51, 59) left Front sts on holder.

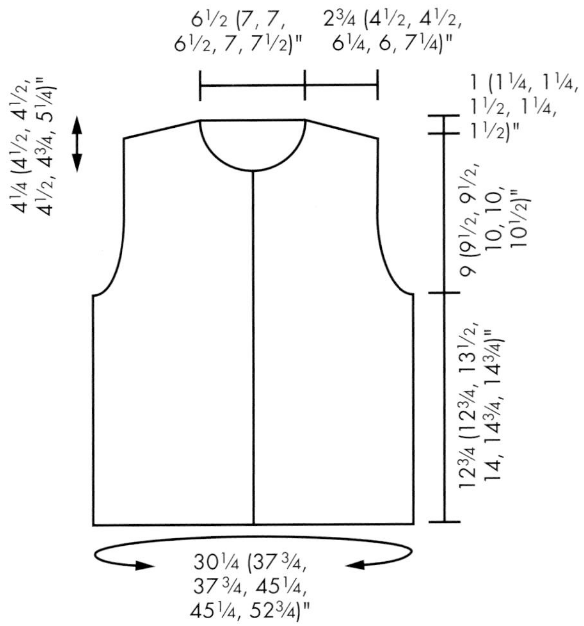
6½ (7, 7, 6½, 7, 7½)"
2¾ (4½, 4½, 6¼, 6, 7¼)"
1 (1¼, 1¼, 1½, 1¼, 1½)"
4¼ (4½, 4½, 4½, 4¾, 5¼)"
9 (9½, 9½, 10, 10, 10½)"
12¾ (12¾, 13½, 14, 14¾, 14¾)"
30¼ (37¾, 37¾, 45¼, 45¼, 52¾)"

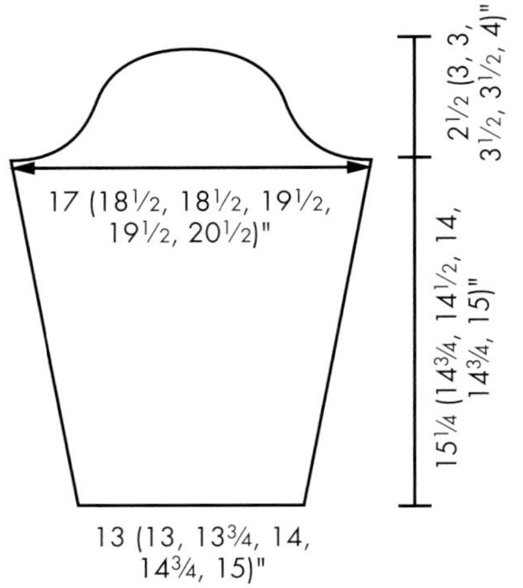
2½ (3, 3, 3½, 3½, 4)"
17 (18½, 18½, 19½, 19½, 20½)"
15¼ (14¾, 14½, 14, 14¾, 15)"
13 (13, 13¾, 14, 14¾, 15)"

BACK ARMHOLE SHAPING

Working only with Back sts, work Armhole shaping as foll: BO 2 (2, 2, 4, 4, 4) sts at beg of next 2 rows, then BO 2 (2, 2, 2, 2, 3) sts at beg of next 4 rows—56 (74, 74, 86, 86, 100) sts rem.

Cont working Chart D as est across rem Back sts until Armhole measures 9 (9½, 9½, 10, 10, 10½)" (23 [24, 24, 25.5, 25.5, 26.5] cm.) End with a WS row.

SHOULDER SHAPING

BO 5 (5, 5, 8, 7, 9) sts at beg of next 2 rows, then BO 4 (8, 8, 10, 10, 12) sts at start of next 4 rows. BO rem 30 (32, 32, 30, 32, 34) sts for back Neck.

FRONT ARMHOLE SHAPING

Working on 34 (42, 42, 51, 51, 59) Front sts, and using two balls of yarn, work both sides at once as follows: BO 2 (2, 2, 4, 4, 4) sts at Armhole edge once, then BO 2 (2, 2, 2, 2, 3) sts at Armhole edge twice—28 (36, 36, 43, 43, 49) sts rem on each Front.

Cont working Chart D as est across rem Front sts until Armhole measures 5¾ (6⅛, 6⅛, 7, 6½, 6⅞)" (14.5 [15.5, 15.5, 18, 16.5, 17.5] cm.)

NECK SHAPING

At each Neck edge, working both Fronts at the same time, BO 6 (6, 6, 6, 7, 7) sts once, then BO 1 (1, 1, 1, 1, 1) sts at Neck edge every row 3 times, then BO 2 (2, 2, 2, 2, 2) sts at Neck edge every other row 2 times, then BO 1 (1, 1, 1, 1, 1) sts at Neck edge every fourth row 2 times—13 (21, 21, 28, 27, 33) sts rem in each Shoulder.

Cont working Chart D as est across rem sts until Armhole measures 9 (9½, 9½, 10, 10, 10½)" (23 [24, 24, 25.5, 25.5, 26.5] cm). End with a WS row.

SHAPE SHOULDERS

BO 5 (5, 5, 8, 7, 9) sts at Armhole edge once, then BO 4 (8, 8, 10, 10, 12) sts at Armhole edge twice.

SLEEVES (MAKE 2)

With smaller needle, CO 49 (53, 53, 57, 57, 61) sts.

Knit 2 rows.

Work Rows 1–6 of Chart A once.

Work Rows 1–4 of Chart C once, dec 1 (0, 0, 0, 0, 0, inc 4) sts in last row of chart—48 (53, 53, 57, 57, 65) sts.

NEXT ROW (RS): Change to larger needle and starting with st 11 (17, 17, 15, 15, 11) of Row 1 of Chart D, work across all sts, placing a marker after each repeat of chart and ending with st 7 (1, 1, 3, 3, 7). Inc 1 st each end every 6 rows 14 (15, 15, 15, 15, 13) times—76 (83, 83, 87, 87, 91) sts.

Work even until Sleeve measures 13 (13, 13¾, 14, 14¾, 15)" (33 [33, 35, 35.5, 37.5, 38] cm from eyelet row. End with a WS row.

CAP SHAPING

BO 7 (7, 7, 8, 8, 8) sts at beg of next 6 rows, then BO 3
(4, 4, 3, 3, 3) sts at beg of next 4 rows, then BO 2 (3, 2,
3, 2, 3) sts at beg of next 2 (2, 4, 4, 4, 4) rows.
BO rem 18 (19, 17, 15, 19, 19) sts.

FINISHING

Block all pieces. Sew Sleeves into Armholes, sew
underarm and side seams. If the Shoulder droops a little
down the arm, turn sweater inside out and work a row of
slip stitch crochet along shoulder seams to tighten them
up and slightly shirr (gather) the seam.

NECK

With smaller needle PU&K 65 (65, 69, 69, 73, 73) sts
around Neck opening.
Knit 2 rows.
Work Rows 1–6 of Chart A once.
BO all sts *loosely*. Sew bound-off edge to wrong side of
Neck opening where sts were picked up.

PLACKETS

With smaller needle (circ), PU&K 70 (70, 74, 74, 79,
79) sts up right Front edge, including along the edge of
neck binding.
Knit 2 rows.
Work Rows 1–6 of Chart A once.
BO all sts *loosely*. Sew bound-off edge to wrong side of
right Front where sts were picked up.
Repeat for left Front Placket.

BELT

Create a 60" (152.5 cm) piece of I-cord (or longer, if
desired) and thread through the series of eyelet holes that
falls nearest your natural waist. Tie loosely
like a negligee to wear.

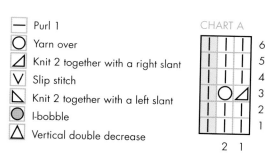

	Purl 1
O	Yarn over
◿	Knit 2 together with a right slant
V	Slip stitch
◺	Knit 2 together with a left slant
●	I-bobble
△	Vertical double decrease

CHART B

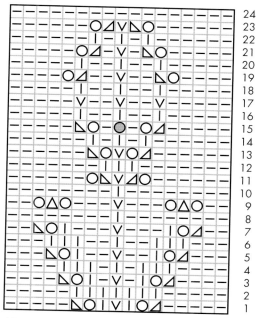

CHART C

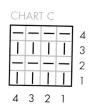

CHART A

CHART D

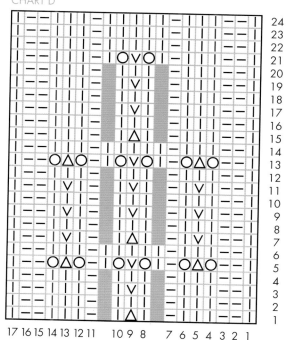

Charade

A convertible is sexy, a convertible wrap cardigan is stylish, flattering, *and* sexy! This surplice top features all-over lattice lace patterning and the fronts are extended so you can tie them in front. You can also pull the fronts around to the back and tie them for a ballet-inspired feeling. Ribbon yarn in this top drapes beautifully.

Skill Level
ADVANCED

SIZE
To fit bust: 30 (40, 50)" (76 [101.5, 127] cm)

FINISHED MEASUREMENTS
Bust (wrapped with ease): 34 (44, 54)" (86 [112, 137] cm)

Hem (unwrapped): 91¼ (121¼, 141¼)" (231.8 [308, 384.2] cm)

Length: 30½ (31½, 32½)" (77.5 [80, 82.5] cm)

MATERIALS
Zen by Berroco (1¾ oz [50 g] balls, each approx 111 yds [101 m], 60% nylon, 40% cotton), Shiseido Blue 8241, 7 (9, 10) balls or 758 (826, 960) yds (684 [753.5, 875.5] m) worsted weight ribbon yarn

Size 6 (4 mm) needle 36" (91 cm) long

Size 8 (5 mm) needle 36" (91 cm) long, or size to obtain gauge

Size G/6 (4 mm) crochet hook

Darning needle

Stitch holders

Stitch markers, including two markers in contrasting colors

GAUGE
4 sts and 6.5 rows = 1" (2.5 cm) over Lattice Lace Pat (Chart A) using larger needle

It is essential to work a rather large swatch containing at least 2 repeats of the 15-st Lattice Lace Pat in Chart A. Refer to glossary on page 136 for: 3-needle BO, K2togL, K2togR, K3togL, Long Tail Cast-On, and YO.

BODY
With larger needle and A, using the long-tail method cast on 365 (485, 605) sts.

Note: Use one strand from each of 2 separate balls of yarn to make this easier. Cut one strand of yarn at end of CO.

Knit 1 row.

NEXT ROW (RS): K1, (k2togR, YO); rep to end of row, end k1.

NEXT ROW (WS): Knit.

NEXT ROW (RS): Work Row 1 of Chart B, place contrasting marker (pcm), k2, (work Row 1 of Chart A, pm) 9 (12, 15) times, place a double marker to note right side of garment, (work Row 1 of Chart A, pm) 4 (6, 8) times, place a double marker to note left side of garment, (work Row 1 of Chart A, pm) 9 (12, 15) times, k3, pcm, work Row 1 of Chart C.

NEXT ROW (WS): Work in pats as est.

NEXT ROW (RS): Work Chart B as est, slip contrasting marker (scm), k3togL, work in Chart A as est, slipping side markers as you pass them, to 2 sts before contrasting marker, k2togR, sm, work Chart C as est.

NEXT ROW (WS): Work Chart C as est, p3tog, p to 2 sts before next contrasting marker, slipping side markers as you pass them. P2togL, scm, work Chart B as est.

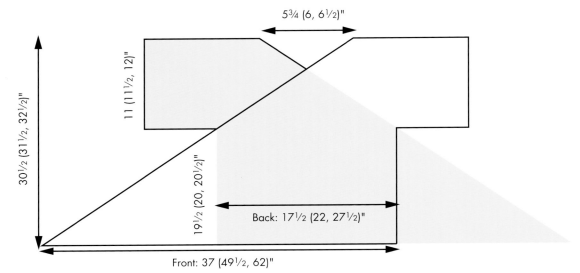

5¾ (6, 6½)"

11 (11½, 12)"

30½ (31½, 32½)"

19½ (20, 20½)"

Back: 17½ (22, 27½)"

Front: 37 (49½, 62)"

Total Body Width at Bottom: 91¼ (121¼, 151¼)"

Note: When working decreases at contrasting marker every right-side row, be sure to omit YOs if the corresponding k2tog will not be worked and vice versa.

Rep last 2 rows, dec 2 sts after first contrasting marker and dec 1 before second contrasting marker every row until piece measures 19½ (20, 20½)" (50 [51.3, 52.6] cm) from cast-on edge. End with a WS row.

ARMHOLE DIVIDE

NEXT ROW (RS): Work as est, cont with dec at contrasting marker to double marker. Slip sts just worked (Right Front) to holder to work later. Cont with Back sts, work in pat as est to next double marker. Join second ball of yarn and work rem sts in row, dec at contrasting marker and working edge sts as est. Slip this last group of sts (Left Front) to holder to work later.

BACK

NEXT ROW (WS): Returning to Back sts, CO 30 sleeve sts, work across 60 (90, 120) Back sts in charted pat as est, CO 30 sleeve sts—120 (150, 180) sts.
NEXT ROW (RS): Knit new CO sts, work Back sts in pat as est, cont in pat as est across last newly cast-on 30 sts for sleeve.
NEXT ROW (WS): Work across new CO sts in pat as est, work across Back, then cont on to left sleeve cast-on sts, incorporating new sts into pat as est across Back. Work even, incorporating new sts into pat as est and

with no shaping until piece measures 11 (11½, 12)" (28.2 [29.5, 30.8] cm) from armhole divide.
End with a RS row and slip sts to holder to work 3-needle BO at shoulders later.

FRONTS

Working both Fronts at the same time using separate balls of yarn, add sts for left and right sleeves as follows: Return to Fronts sts and CO 30 sts at each armhole edge.

LEFT FRONT

NEXT ROW (RS): Work across all sts, dec at neck edge and working in pat as est.
NEXT ROW (WS): Work to Armhole edge, CO 30 sts.
NEXT ROW (RS): Work in St st across CO sts, work across rem sts in pat as est—decreasing at neck edge.
NEXT ROW (WS): Work CO sts, work across new left sleeve sts in pat as est.
Cont working sleeve in pat as est for Left Front, dec at neck edge as est.

RIGHT FRONT

NEXT ROW (RS): Dec at neck edge as est and work across all sts in pat as est, CO 30 sts.
NEXT ROW (WS): Work in pat as est across all sts to neck edge.
NEXT ROW (RS): Dec at neck edge as est and work across all sts, incorporating sleeve sts into pat as est.

NEXT ROW (WS): Work in pat as est to neck edge. Cont working sleeve in pat as est for Right and Left Fronts, dec at neck edges as est until 58 (59, 60) sts rem at Right Front and 59 (60, 61) sts rem at Left Front. Work one more row, dec 1 st at Left Front—58 (59, 60) sts rem each Front. Work even until Front measures same as Back, end with a RS row.

JOINING

Slip lace neck edge sts to holder.

Starting at sleeve edges, with WS tog, join Fronts to Back using 3-needle BO.

BO 26 (28, 30) at center Back.

Return to Front lace edge and cont working in pats as est until both sides reach center Back (end right lace neck edge with a RS row, and left lace neck edge with a WS row). With WS tog, join with a 3-needle BO. Sew bottom edge of lace to Back neck opening.

FINISHING

Weave in ends. Steam-block.

Wear garment by tying long ends in front, or pulling them around the back and tying them, ballet style.

⊿ Knit 2 together with a right slant   ◯ Yarn over

◣ Knit 2 together with a left slant   — Purl 1

| Knit 1   � Knit 3 together with a left slant

◢ Knit 3 together with a right slant

CHART A
LATTICE LACE

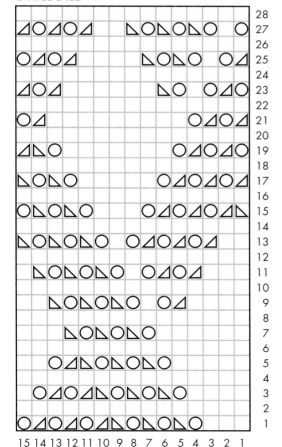

15 14 13 12 11 10 9 8 7 6 5 4 3 2 1

CHART B
RIGHT EDGE

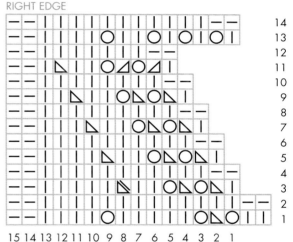

15 14 13 12 11 10 9 8 7 6 5 4 3 2 1

CHART C
LEFT EDGE

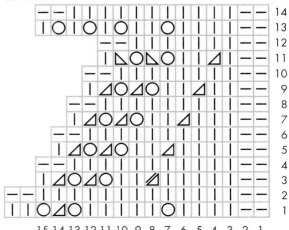

15 14 13 12 11 10 9 8 7 6 5 4 3 2 1

A Room with a View

The look of a late-seventeenth-century Restoration bodice, the ease of a T-shirt, and the flattering fit that only surplice shaping can give. This lace peplum surplice design is excellent for all body types, especially a short-waisted figure. The body and sleeves of this faux-cardigan are knit first, with the hem and cuffs picked up and knit later in some of the easiest lace you'll ever work!

Skill Level
INTERMEDIATE

SIZE
To fit bust: 28 (32, 36, 40, 44, 54)" (71 [81, 91, 101.5, 112, 127] cm)

FINISHED MEASUREMENTS
Bust: 32 (36, 40, 44, 48, 54)" (81 [91, 101.5, 112, 122, 137.2] cm)

Length: 17½ (18, 19¼, 20¼, 22, 23¼)" (44.5 [45.5, 49, 51.5, 56, 59] cm)

MATERIALS
Vintage Cotton by Karabella (1¾ oz [50 g] balls, each approx 140 yds [128 m], 100% mercerized cotton)

A: French Blue 319, 4 (5, 5, 6, 6, 7) balls or 596 (657, 713, 774, 843, 930) yds (543.5 [593, 650.5, 706, 769, 848] m) sportweight yarn

B: White 356, 2 (2, 2, 2, 3, 3) balls or 255 (279, 306, 332, 361, 399) yds (232.5 [254.5, 279, 303, 329, 364] m) sportweight yarn

Size 5 (3.75) mm circular needles at least 24" (61 cm) long, or size to obtain gauge.

See Circular Stress page 112 for thoughts on circular needle lengths.

Stitch markers

Stitch holders

Darning needle

GAUGE
4.75 sts and 6 rows = 1" (2.5 cm) ribbing/seed pattern, slightly stretched

Refer to glossary on page 136 for: K2tog Picot Bind-Off, K2togL, K2togR, m1, and YO.

RIBBING/SEED PATTERN
See Chart A if you prefer to work from charts.

Worked over an even number of sts.

ROW 1 (RS): (K1, p1); rep across all sts.

ROW 2 (WS): Knit.

Rep Rows 1 and 2 for pat.

Note: Due to shaping in the garment body, k1, p1 rib on RS rows will stagger, forming a garter/seed st—see Chart A for a visual reference.

BODY
With B and a provisional cast-on, cast on 152 (172, 192, 208, 228, 256) sts.

NEXT ROW (RS): K6, place marker (pm), k76 (86, 96, 104, 114, 128) sts, pm, k to end of row.

NEXT ROW (WS): Knit.

NEXT ROW (RS): K2, m1, *k1, p1; rep from * to last 4 sts, k2togR, k2.

NEXT ROW (WS): P2, k to last 2 sts, p2.
Rep last 2 rows, inc at start and dec at end of RS rows until piece measures 5½ (5½, 6, 6½, 7, 7)" (14.1 [14, 15.25, 16.5, 18, 18] cm) from cast-on edge.

ARMHOLE DIVIDE

NEXT ROW (RS): Working inc and dec as est, work to first marker. Slip sts just worked to holder to work later for right Front. Cont with Back sts, working in pat as est to next marker. Slip rem sts to holder to work later for left Front.

BACK

Cont working even in pat with no shaping until piece measures 7 (7⅜, 7⅞, 8, 8¾, 9¼)" (18 [18.7, 20, 20.5, 22.5, 23.4] cm). Slip sts to holder to work later.

FRONTS

Cont to work shaping for Fronts as est until the same number of sts rem for both Fronts—38 (43, 48, 52, 57, 64) sts. Cont shaping left Front as est, beg dec right Front as for left Front. Cont dec until 8 (12, 14, 17, 20, 24) sts rem for each Front.

Work even with no further shaping until piece measures same as Back, then work even for an additional 1 (1¼, 1¼, 1½, 1½, 2)" (2.5 [3, 3, 3.8, 3.8, 5] cm). Join

Detail of lace hem.

Fronts to Back with a 3-needle BO, leaving center 34 (34, 36, 36, 36, 38) sts live on a piece of waste yarn to work later.

SLEEVES (MAKE 2)

With A, PU&K 72 (76, 80, 84, 92, 96) sts around Armhole opening. Place marker to note start of round (center underarm).

Work in St st for 10 rows, then dec as follows:
ROUND 1: K1, k2togL, k to end of round.
ROUNDS 2 AND 4: Knit all sts.
ROUND 3: K to 3 sts before marker, k2togR, k1.
Rep last 4 rounds 30 (30, 32, 34, 38, 38) times total, until 42 (46, 48, 50, 54, 58) sts rem. Work even until Sleeve measures 9 (9½, 10¼, 10½, 11½, 12¼)" (23 [24, 26, 26.5, 29, 31] cm).

CUFF

Change to B.

Working in the round, work Chart B Rows 1–9, then rep Rows 5–9 until Cuff measures 3 (3¼, 3½, 3½, 3¾, 4)" (7.5 [8.3, 9, 9, 9.5, 10] cm) or desired length. BO all sts loosely with k2tog picot BO.

FINISHING

Sew Fronts together along diagonal edge. Weave in ends.

With B, PU&K 42 (44, 46, 48, 52, 56) sts starting 1" (2.5 cm) below Front crossover and continuing up right neck to center Back. Then PU&K 106 (108, 116, 122, 132, 140) sts down left neck to bottom of left Front—148 (152, 162, 170, 184, 196) sts.

Work 6 rows in garter st.

Work k2tog picot BO all sts.

PEPLUM LACE

With B, PU 152 (172, 192, 208, 228, 256) provisionally cast-on sts at bottom of garment and join. Working in the round, work Chart B Rows 1–9, then rep Rows 5–9 until Peplum measures 7½ (8, 8½, 8¾, 9½, 10¼)" (19.2 [20.5, 21.8, 22.4, 24.4, 26.3] cm) or to desired length. BO all sts loosely with k2tog picot BO.

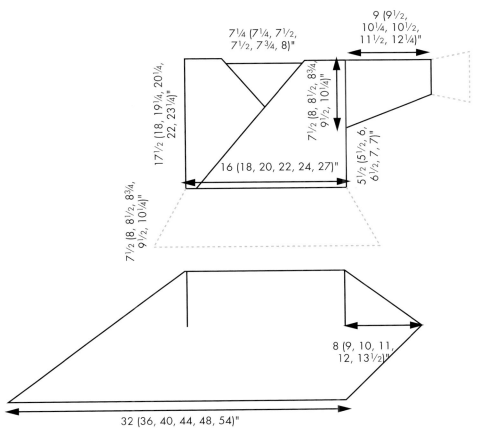

7¼ (7¼, 7½, 7½, 7¾, 8)"

9 (9½, 10¼, 10½, 11½, 12¼)"

17½ (18, 19¼, 20¼, 22, 23¼)"

7½ (8, 8½, 9½, 10¼)"

7½ (8, 8½, 9½, 10¼)"

16 (18, 20, 22, 24, 27)"

5½ (5½, 6, 6½, 7, 7)"

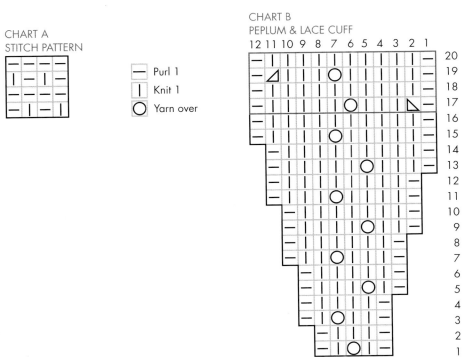

8 (9, 10, 11, 12, 13½)"

32 (36, 40, 44, 48, 54)"

CHART A
STITCH PATTERN

— Purl 1

| Knit 1

◯ Yarn over

CHART B
PEPLUM & LACE CUFF

12 11 10 9 8 7 6 5 4 3 2 1

20
19
18
17
16
15
14
13
12
11
10
9
8
7
6
5
4
3
2
1

4 3   2 1

Notorious

Some shapes deserve their moment in the sun—and this sweater shines with fitted detail! Ribbed sides and back emphasize the front waist shaping, exaggerating the curve of the hip and the bust. Horizontal I-cord adds a hint of underwire shaping, with a crochet neck edging, twisted cord bust detail, and knit-on drape sleeves worthy of a committed knitter. Loosen the front ties for a modest look, or tie them tight to create the illusion of cleavage. This project is not so much *difficult* as it is *complex*. Break it down, take it step by step, and conquer the sweetheart neckline corset!

Skill Level
ADVANCED

SIZE
To fit bust: 25½ (34, 38½, 43, 51½, 56)" (65.5 [87, 98.5, 110.5, 132, 143.5] cm)

FINISHED MEASUREMENTS
Bust: 26½ (35, 39½, 44, 52½, 57)" (67.5 [89, 100, 112, 133.5, 145] cm)

Length: 22¾ (23¾, 24, 25, 26¼, 27½)" (58 [60, 61, 63.5, 66.5, 70] cm)

MATERIALS
Touché by Berroco (1¾ oz [50 g] skeins, each approx 89 yds [82 m] per skein, 50% cotton, 50% Modal® rayon)

A: Lemon Meringue 7914, 4 (5, 5, 5, 6, 7) skeins or 331 (414, 446, 482, 547, 587) yds (302 [377.5, 407, 439.5, 499, 535.5] m) worsted weight yarn

B: Green Tea 7930, 1 (1, 1, 1, 1, 1) skein or 73 (91, 98, 106, 121, 129) yds (66.5 [83, 89.5, 96.5, 109.5, 117.5] m) worsted weight yarn

Size 6 (4 mm) circular needle at least 24" (61 cm) long

Size 7 (4.5 mm) circular needle at least 24" (61 cm) long, or size to obtain gauge

Size 8 (5 mm) circular needle at least 24" (61 cm) long

Size F/5 (3.75 mm) crochet hook

Darning needle

Stitch markers

GAUGE
4 sts and 6 rows = 1" (2.5 cm) over k2, p2 rib using size 7 needle

Refer to glossary on page 136 for: C4L, C4R, CCO, DKSS, I-Cord Horizontal Stripe, K2togL, K2togR, K2tog Picot BO, PU&K, Twisted Cord, VDD, W&T, and YO.

BODY

With A and largest needle, cast on 117 (157, 177, 197, 237, 257) sts. Join, placing marker to note start of round.

NEXT ROUND: Work Row 1 of Chart A (Center Cable) across 17 sts between markers, then work Row 1 of Chart B (Rib) around rem sts 5 (7, 8, 9, 11, 12) times.

NEXT ROUND: Work Row 2 of Chart A between markers as est, work in rib as est around all rem sts.

Cont working in rib as est, slipping markers in each round and working center 17 sts in Chart A, until ribbing measures 1" (2.5 cm) from cast-on round.

Cont with 17 center sts in cable as est and work Rows 1 and 2 of Chart C (Bias Nondecrease Panel) around rem sts until piece measures 5½ (5½, 5¾, 5¾, 6, 6¼)" (14 [14, 14.5, 14.5, 15, 16] cm) from cast-on. End with Round 4 of Chart C.

WAIST SHAPING

NEXT ROUND: Work 17 center sts in Chart A as est, sm, work Row 1 of Chart D (Bias Decrease Panel) across next 20 sts (shaping panel), pm, rep Row 1 of Chart C 3 (5, 6, 7, 9, 10) times, pm, work Row 1 of Chart D across last 20 sts (shaping panel).

Work center panel in cable as est and cont in Charts C and D as est, working shaping only in panels on either side of cable with no shaping around sides and Back. Dec in shaping panels only as directed in chart to Row 18 of Chart D—101 (141, 161, 181, 221, 241) sts rem. Work even, rep Rows 17 and 18 of Chart D in shaping panels with no further decreasing until piece measures 8⅝ (8⅝, 8¾, 8¾, 8⅞, 9)" (22 [22, 22.2, 22.2, 22.5, 23] cm) from cast-on edge.

UPPER WAIST SHAPING

Cont with Chart D in shaping panels and working 17 cable sts and sides and Back as est, work to Row 36 of Chart D—117 (157, 177, 197, 237, 257) sts. Cont working with no further shaping, rep Rows 1 and 2 of Chart C around all noncable sts, until piece measures 18¾ (19¼, 19½, 20, 20¾, 21½)" (47.5 [49, 49.5, 51, 53, 54.5] cm) from cast-on (or desired length to Armholes). End with an even round, removing all markers in last round except for marker noting start of round.

DIVIDE FOR FRONT AND BACK

NEXT ROUND: Work 17 center sts in cable as est, work 21 (31, 36, 41, 51, 56) sts in Chart C as est, place double marker (right underarm), work 58 (78, 88, 98, 118, 128) sts in pats as est to 21 (31, 36, 41, 51, 56) sts before end of round, turn work.

From this point work back and forth in rows. Note that when working a partial chart rep, omit YOs if the corresponding k2tog will not be worked and vice versa.

Notorious neckline with twisted cord tucked in.

NEXT ROW (WS): Work in charted pat as est to double marker, turn work.

BACK ARMHOLE SHAPING

Cont in pat as est, BO 5 (7, 8, 9, 11, 12) sts at start of next 2 rows, then dec 1 st at each edge of every row 8 (11, 12, 14, 17, 18) times—32 (42, 48, 52, 62, 68) sts rem across back.

Work even until piece measures 3½ (4, 4, 4½, 5, 5½)" (9 [10, 10, 11.5, 12.5, 14] cm from start of Armhole shaping.

RUFFLED CROCHET EDGING

With B and crochet hook, work k2tog picot BO across all sts, working 3 chains between each BO st. Do not break yarn. You will have a chain 3-space for each bound-off st, the BO edge will look ruffled.

Turn work. *Working from WS to RS, insert hook into next chain 3-space, working from RS to WS, bring hook back through next chain 3-space; rep from * for next 2 chain 3-spaces—4 chain 3-spaces are resting on hook. Draw a loop through all 4 chain spaces, chain 4 sts, rep from * across rem ch spaces.
Fasten off.

FRONT ARMHOLE AND BUST SHAPING

Removing each marker as you come to it across the Front, work horizontal I-cord across Front 59 (79, 89, 99, 119, 129) sts as follows:

(K1 between next 2 sts on needle, k2, k2togL, slip 3 sts from right-hand needle back onto left-hand needle); rep until all sts have been worked, ending with k2togL before double marker—59 (79, 89, 99, 119, 129) sts across Front.

NEXT ROW (WS): K29 (39, 44, 49, 59, 64) sts, p1, k to end of row.

NEXT ROW (RS): PU&K edge st from right end of I-cord 2 rows below, purl next st on needle, PU&K from I-cord st next to one just picked up (inc of 2 sts), p2, k to 1 st before center (knit) st, YO, VDD, YO, knit to last 3 sts, p2, PU&K edge st from left edge of I-cord, p1, PU&K from I-cord next st to one just picked up (inc of 2 sts)—63 (83, 93, 103, 123, 133) sts.

NEXT ROW (WS): Wyif sl 1, k1, wyif sl 1, k2, purl to last 5 sts, k2, wyif sl 1, k1, wyif sl 1.

NEXT ROW (RS): K1, wyif sl 1, k1, knit to 1 st before center st, YO, VDD, YO, knit to last 5 sts, p2, k1, wyif sl 1, k1.Rep last 2 rows until piece measures 6 (7¼, 7¾, 8½, 10, 10¾)" (15 [18.5, 19.5, 21.5, 25.5, 27.5] cm) from middle of horizontal I-cord band. End with a WS row. Work Ruffled Crochet Edging across all sts as for Back, working last ruffle with fewer than 3 chain spaces if necessary.

SLEEVES (MAKE 2)

With B and smallest needle, PU&K 23 (22, 22, 25, 27, 29) sts up Front Armhole edge, cable cast on 20 (30, 30, 34, 34, 38) sts, PU&K 17 (16, 16, 17, 19, 21) sts down Back Armhole edge—60 (68, 68, 76, 80, 88)

NEXT ROW (WS): Wyif sl 1, k1, wyif sl 1, k2 (DKSS edge), *k2, p2 rep from * to last 5 sts, k2, wyif sl 1, k1, wyif sl 1 (DKSS edge).

NEXT ROW (RS): K1, wyif sl 1, k1, p2 (DKSS edge), work 27 (31, 31, 35, 37, 41) sts in pat as est, W&T.

NEXT ROW (WS): Work 4 sts, W&T.

NEXT ROW: Work to 3 st past last wrapped st, W&T. Change to medium needle. Rep last row, slipping wraps

up to needle and working together with wrapped st, until all sts are worked, ending with a RS row.

NEXT ROW (WS): Work 32 (36, 36, 40, 42, 46) in pat as est, W&T.

NEXT ROW (RS): Work 4 sts, W&T.

NEXT ROW: Work to 3 sts past last wrapped st, W&T. Change to largest needle. Rep last row until all sts are worked at each edge, end with a WS row.

Knit 2 rows.

BO all sts loosely.

FINISHING

Weave in ends.

Create a 40" (101.5 cm) finished piece of 2-color twisted cord using A and B. Starting at the top center front, weave strand down through right Front bust eyelets, then weave through loose sts under left cup. Rep with other end of cord, weaving through left bust eyelets and under right bust.

With a darning needle, tack edges of cord to inner sides of corset.

Pull cord tight, gathering center Front bust, and tie in a bow (you can cut and knot the ends of the cord or leave it in a loop or tuck it in as shown in the detail).

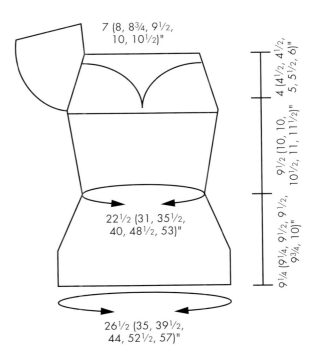

7 (8, 8¾, 9½, 10, 10½)"

4 (4½, 4½, 5, 5½, 6)"

9½ (10, 10, 11, 11½)"

10½ (11, 11, 11½)"

22½ (31, 35½, 40, 48½, 53)"

9¼ (9¼, 9½, 9½, 9¾, 10)"

26½ (35, 39½, 44, 52½, 57)"

CHART A   CENTER CABLE
(work only across center 17 sts)

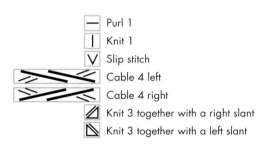

17 16 15 14 13 12 11 10 9 8 7 6 5 4 3 2 1

CHART B   RIB
(work across all noncenter Cable Chart sts)

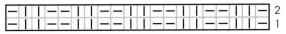

CHART C   BIAS NONDECREASE PANEL
(repeat these 2 rows in all nondecreasing bias panels)

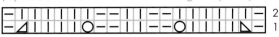

CHART D   BIAS DECREASE PANEL CHART
(work only in panels on either side of center front Cable Chart)

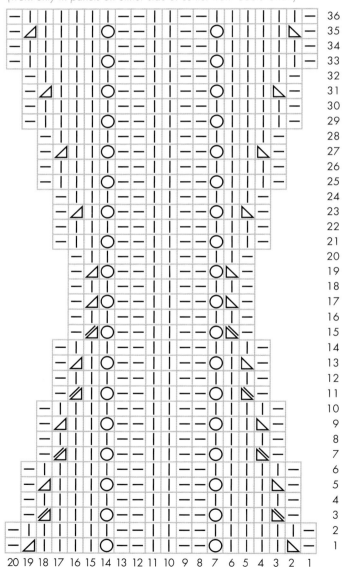

20 19 18 17 16 15 14 13 12 11 10 9 8 7 6 5 4 3 2 1

—	Purl 1
		Knit 1
V	Slip stitch
	Cable 4 left
	Cable 4 right
	Knit 3 together with a right slant
	Knit 3 together with a left slant

Basic Crochet Techniques

Crochet is used throughout this book for edging, to create an interesting bind-off, or to make a collar. If we think of knitting as creating fabric from loops of yarn using two needles, crochet is simply making a similar fabric using only one needle (hook), whereby we bind off each stitch as we work it. I feel that it is vital for all knitters to embrace the basics of crochet to move their knitting to a higher level, and to gain a deeper understanding of knitting! Everything we learn makes our lives and our knitting richer and deeper.

CHAINING (CH)

The first step to most crochet pieces is to create a chain of stitches.

STEP 1 Create a slipknot, insert the crochet hook into the loop of the slipknot.

STEP 2 Holding both the tail and the live end of the yarn in your left hand, wrap the live end around the hook and pull this loop through the slipknot loop.

STEP 3 You have just created a chain stitch.

STEP 4 Repeat Steps 1 and 2 to create a chain of stitches.

SINGLE CROCHET (SC)

After creating a crochet chain, work one more stitch and, skipping this stitch, insert the hook into the second stitch from the hook.

STEP 5 Draw a loop of yarn through this stitch. There will now be two loops on the hook.

STEP 6 Wrap the yarn around the hook and draw this loop through both loops already on the hook.

Repeat Steps 5 and 6 with each stitch, working back to the original slipknot.

STEP NEXT ROW Turn work, make 1 chain st (ch 1) and repeat steps 5 and 6 across the work, inserting the hook into both legs of each stitch from the previous row.

SL ST

Slip crochet hook into st, YO, draw loop through st and through loop on hook.

HALF DOUBLE CROCHET (HDC)

Yarn over hook. Insert hook in the next stitch to be worked. Yarn over hook. Pull yarn through stitch. Yarn over hook. Pull yarn through all 3 loops on hook (one half double crochet made).

DOUBLE CROCHET (DC)

YO hook, insert hook in the next stitch to be worked, YO hook, draw through stitch, YO hook, draw through first 2 loops on hook, YO hook, draw through remaining 2 loops on hook.

TRIPLE OR TREBLE CROCHET (TR)

YO twice, insert hook in the next stitch to be worked, YO, draw yarn through stitch—3 loops on hook, YO, draw through first 2 loops on hook, YO, draw through first 2 loops on hook, YO, draw through remaining 2 loops on hook.

Casablanca

A flattering top for every figure type! Worked from the top down with "afterthought" sleeves, this lace panel corset top is basically a tube with lace in the front and ribbing at the sides and back. The construction makes it easy to try this on as you work so you can knit it as long or short as you like. Crocheted edging around the top draws in the neckline for a sophisticated fit.

Skill Level
INTERMEDIATE

SIZE

To fit bust: 28 (40, 52)" (71 [101.5, 132] cm)

FINISHED MEASUREMENTS

Neck Opening: approx 28 (40, 52)" (71 [101.5, 132] cm), exact size determined by tension of crochet edging

Bust: 30 (42, 54)" (76 [106.5, 137] cm)

Length: 22¾ (23¾, 24¾)" (58 [60, 63] cm)

MATERIALS

Zodiac by Karabella (1¾ oz [50g] balls, each approx 98 yds [90 m], 100% mercerized cotton), Sage Green 413, 7 (9, 11) balls

Size 5 (3.75 mm) circular needle at least 24" (61 cm) long, and 12" (30.5 cm) long

Size 6 (4 mm) circular needle 12" (30.5 cm) long

Size 7 (4.5 mm) circular needles at least 24" (61 cm) long, and 12" (30.5 cm) long

Stitch markers

Size F/5 (3.75 mm) crochet hook

Darning needle

GAUGE

5 sts and 6 rows = 1" (2.5 cm) in rib slightly stretched using size 5 needle, or size to obtain gauge

Refer to glossary on page 136 for: K2togL, K2togR, Sl st, PU&K, VDD, W&T, and YO. See page 47 for crochet technique: Single Crochet (SC), Sl st.

NECKLINE

With smallest 24" needle, CO 150 (210, 270) sts. Join, making sure not to twist sts on needle.

Knit 1 round.

Purl 1 round.

NEXT ROUND: Work Row 1 of Chart A (Scalloped Edge) around all sts 10 (14, 18) times. Place a contrasting marker to note start of round.

NEXT ROUND: Work Row 2 of Chart A around all sts. Rep last 2 rounds 2 more times—6 rounds of Chart A.

NEXT 7 ROUNDS: Change to largest 24" needle and work Rows 1–7 of Chart B (Lace Panel Corset Edge) around all sts.

ARMHOLES

NEXT ROUND: Working Row 8 of Chart B, create Armhole placement as follows:

K9 (23, 30) sts. With a piece of waste yarn, k28 (29, 30) sts (right Armhole). Slip these waste-yarn-worked sts back to left-hand needle and work them again with the sweater yarn.

K46 (76, 105) sts (Back).

With a piece of waste yarn, k28 (29, 30) sts (left

Detail of Casablanca neckline.

Armhole). Slip these waste-yarn-worked sts back to left-hand needle and work them again with the sweater yarn. K9 (23, 30) sts.

Place marker, k30 (30, 45) sts.

You now have 30 (30, 45) sts in the center front panel between markers and 120 (180, 225) sts outside of markers.

BODY

NEXT ROUND: Work Chart D (Rib) 8 (12, 15) times around corset sides and back, then work Chart C (Lace Panel), 2 (2, 3) times across center front sts between markers.

Cont working charts as est until piece measures 18½ (19½, 20½)" (47 [49.5, 52] cm) from Armhole waste yarn, ending with Row 8 or 18 of Chart C.

HEM

Work Rows 1 and 2 of Chart A around all sts twice (4 rounds total), then work Rows 1–8 of Chart B once (8 more rounds). Knit 1 round, purl 1 round, then BO all sts loosely.

SLEEVES (MAKE 2)

With smallest 12" needle, pick up all sts above and below waste yarn—28 (29, 30) sts at the neck side and 29 (30, 31) sts at the body side of the waste yarn.

Pick up an additional 2 sts on either edge of the Armhole opening to close the gap created when moving from upper to lower sts in opening (mark any one of these sts with a safety pin)—61 (63, 65) sts total. Remove waste yarn. Slip sts onto largest 12" needle, arranging them so you are starting at the center st on the neck side of the opening (15 [15, 16] sts from Sleeve edge where the st is marked with a safety pin). This center st is the center top st of the Sleeve cap.

CAP SHAPING

ROW 1 (RS): Starting at center top and working center st as st 8 of Chart D (Rib) work 2 sts (working Chart D sts 8 and 9), W&T.

ROW 2 (WS): Work in rib back to center st, then cont in charted pat, work 2 sts, W&T.

ROW 3 (RS): Cont in chart pat as est, working to next wrapped st, lift wrap to needle and work tog with wrapped st, then cont in chart working 3 sts, W&T.

ROW 4 (WS): Cont in chart pat as est, working to next wrapped st, lift wrap to needle and work tog with wrapped st, then cont in chart working 3 sts, W&T.

ROW 5 (RS): Cont in chart pat as est, working to next wrapped st, lift wrap to needle and work tog with wrapped st, then cont in chart, working 2 sts, W&T.

ROW 6 (WS): Cont in chart pat as est, working to next wrapped st, lift wrap to needle and work tog with wrapped st, then cont in chart working 2 sts, W&T.

NEXT ROW: Cont in chart pat as est, working to next wrapped st, lift wrap to needle and work tog with wrapped st, then cont in chart working 3 (2, 2) sts, W&T. Work last row a total of 2 (4, 4) times, ending with a WS row so you are ready to start a RS row—34 (32, 34) sts rem unworked at Sleeve underarm.

SLEEVE

From this point you will be working the Sleeve in the round. Cont with Sleeve cap after last W&T and, working on the RS of the piece, work across all cap sts to last W&T, work wrap as for previous wrapped sts, pm, k34 (32, 34) sts, pm, work in rib as est to marker.

(K2 [2, 3] sts, m1), 14 (12, 10) times, knit to marker—75 (75, 75) sts.

Beg working Chart B around all sts, matching chart placement with rib st placement around all sts.

Work 8-row rep of chart with smallest 12" needle, then work 8-row rep with medium 12" needle and end by working 8 rows of chart with largest 12" needle.

NEXT ROUND: Knit.

NEXT ROUND: Purl.

BO loosely.

FINISHING

Steam-block piece.

CROCHET EDGING

SC around all sts at neck edge for 2 rounds, then work 1 round of sl st crochet, tightening up the neck opening so the garment sits comfortably. Adjust tension, depending on how wide or narrow you prefer the neck opening.

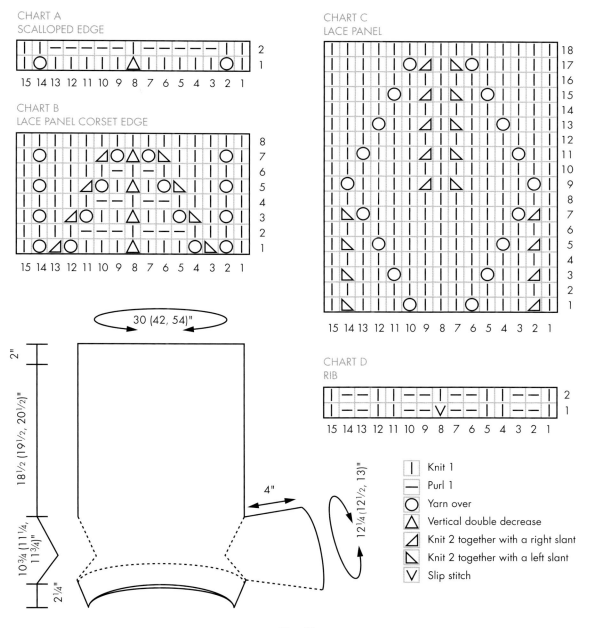

CHART A
SCALLOPED EDGE

CHART B
LACE PANEL CORSET EDGE

CHART C
LACE PANEL

CHART D
RIB

	Knit 1
---	Purl 1
O	Yarn over
△	Vertical double decrease
⟋	Knit 2 together with a right slant
⟍	Knit 2 together with a left slant
V	Slip stitch

Two for the Road

Two lovely yarns join to create one stunning sweater. The body and sleeves are worked in a gullwing, repeating cable pattern, using one strand each of a cotton/wool blend and a laceweight silk/wool yarn. The neck and cuffs are picked up and knit using only the heavier yarn, then an overcollar is knit in lace with the silk and wool. In skin-flattering pinks, this double-layer pullover will become a favorite wardrobe item.

Skill Level
INTERMEDIATE

SIZE
To fit bust: 24 (32, 36, 42, 48, 54)" (61 [81, 91, 106.5, 122, 137] cm)

FINISHED MEASUREMENTS
Bust: 30 (36, 42, 48, 54, 60)" (76 [91, 106.5, 122, 137, 152.5] cm)

Length: 20¾ (21¼, 22, 23, 24¼, 24¾)" (52.5 [54, 56, 58, 61.5, 63] cm)

MATERIALS
A: Dove by Lorna's Laces (2 oz [57 g] skeins, each approx 165 yds [150 m], 80% wool, 20% cotton), Mother Lode 74, 4 (4, 5, 5, 6, 6) skeins or 638 (710, 788, 873, 957, 1038) yds (582 [647.5, 718.5, 796, 873, 946.5] m) sportweight yarn

B: Helen's Lace by Lorna's Laces (4 oz [113 g] skeins, each approx 1250 yds [1140 m] 50% silk, 50% wool), Old Rose 1 (1, 1, 1, 1, 1) skein or 417 (464, 515, 570, 625, 678) yds (380.5 [423, 469.5, 520, 570, 618] m) sportweight yarn

Size 6 (4 mm) circular needle 36" (91 cm) long

Size 8 (5 mm) circular needle 12" (31.5 cm) long

Size 8 (5 mm) circular needle 36" (91 cm) long, or size to obtain gauge

Darning needle

Size 7 (4.5 mm) crochet hook

See Circular Stress page 112 for thoughts on circular needle lengths.

GAUGE
4 sts and 6 rows = 1" (2.5 cm) in Gullwing Cable Pattern using larger needles with one strand of A and B held together

Refer to glossary on page 136 for: C4L, C4R, K2togL, K2togR, K2tog Picot BO, VDD, and YO.

BACK
With larger needle and one strand each of A and B held together, CO 60 (72, 84, 96, 108, 120) sts.

NEXT ROW (RS): Work Row 1 of Chart A (Rib) 10 (12, 14, 16, 18, 20) times across all sts.

NEXT ROW (WS): Work Row 2 of Chart A.

Rep last 2 rows until piece measures 2" (5 cm) from cast-on. End with a WS row.

NEXT ROW (RS): Work Row 1 of Chart B (Double-Layer Gullwing Cable Pattern) 2.5 (3, 3.5, 4, 4.5, 5) times across all sts, ending with st 12 (24, 12, 24, 12, 24) of chart.

Work even until piece measures 12 (12, 12½, 13, 13½, 13½)" (30.8 [30.8, 32.1, 33.3, 34.6, 34.6] cm) from cast-on. End with a WS row.

Two yarns are blended to form the body and sleeves; worked separately at the neck, they create two distinct layers of collar.

ARMHOLE SHAPING

BO 4 (4, 4, 6, 6, 6) sts at beg of next 2 rows, then BO 2 (2, 3, 3, 3, 4) sts at each Armhole edge twice—44 (56, 64, 72, 84, 92) sts rem.

Work even until Armhole measures 8 (8½, 8½, 9, 9½, 10)" (20.5 [21.8, 21.8, 23.1, 24.4, 25.6] cm) from start of shaping. End with a WS row.

SHOULDER SHAPING

BO 4 (6, 7, 8, 9, 11) sts at start of next 4 rows, then BO 4 (6, 7, 8, 10, 11) sts at start of next 2 rows.
BO rem 20 (20, 22, 24, 26, 26) sts.

FRONT

Work as for Back until Armhole measures 5¼ (5½, 5½, 7, 6, 6¾)" (13.5 [14, 14, 18, 15, 17] cm). End with a WS row.

NECK SHAPING

Work 18 (24, 27, 30, 35, 39) sts, join a second ball of A and B, and BO center 8 (8, 10, 12, 14, 14) sts, work rem 18 (24, 27, 30, 35, 39) sts.

Working both Fronts at the same time, BO 1 st at each neck edge every row 1 time, then BO 2 sts at each neck edge every other row 1 time, then BO 3 sts at each neck edge every fourth row 1 time—12 (18, 21, 24, 29, 33) sts rem for each Shoulder.

Work even until neck measures 2¾ (3, 3, 2, 3½, 3¼)" (7.4 [7.4, 7.7, 7.7, 8, 8.3] cm).

SHOULDER SHAPING

BO 4 (6, 7, 8, 9, 11) sts at Armhole edge twice, work 1 row even, then BO rem 4 (6, 7, 8, 11, 11) sts.

SLEEVES (MAKE 2)

With larger needle and one strand each of A and B held together, cast on 2 sts.
NEXT ROW (WS): K2 sts into front and back of both sts—4 sts.
NEXT ROW (RS): K1, yo, k2, yo, k1—6 sts.

NEXT ROW: K1, yo, k4, yo, k1—8 sts.

NEXT ROW: K1, yo, k6, yo, k1—10 sts.

NEXT ROW (WS): K1, yo, k1, work Row 2 of Chart A over next 6 sts, k1, yo, k1—12 sts.

NEXT ROW (RS): K1, yo, p1, k1, work Row 1 of Chart A over next 6 sts, k1 p1, yo, k1—14 sts.

Cont inc 1 st each edge every row by working a YO 1 st in from edge and working new sts into the charted pat as est until 38 (38, 40, 40, 42, 44) sts rem, ending with a WS row.

Work 2 more rows in pats as est with no further inc.

SET UP CABLE PATTERN

Starting with st 18 (18, 17, 17, 16, 15), work Chart B across all sts, ending with st 7 (7, 8, 8, 9, 10).

Note: When there are too few sts to work a cable, work these sts in St st.

Inc 1 st each edge every 6 rows 12 (14, 13, 14, 15, 16) times—62 (66, 66, 68, 72, 76) sts.

Work even in pat as est until piece measures 14¼ (14½, 14¾, 15, 15¾, 16½)" (36.5 [37.2, 37.8, 38.5, 40.4, 42.3] cm) from start of cable pat. End with a WS row.

CAP SHAPING

BO 8 sts at beg of next 2 rows, then BO 4 (4, 4, 4, 5, 5) sts at beg of next 4 rows, then BO 1 (2, 2, 2, 3) sts at beg of next 4 rows, work even with no shaping for 0 (0, 2, 2, 4, 6) rows, then BO 4 sts at start of next 4 rows. BO rem 10 (10, 10, 12, 12, 12) sts.

FINISHING

Block pieces. Sew Sleeves into Armholes. Sew underarm and side seams.

RUFFLED CUFF

With larger 12" circ needle and A, PU&K 40 (40, 50, 50, 50, 50) sts around cuff edge.

NEXT ROUND: (K1, m1); rep to end of round—80 (80, 100, 100, 100, 100) sts.

Purl 1 round.

Knit every round until cuff measures 2 (2, 2½, 3, 3, 3½)" (5 [5, 6.5, 7.5, 7.5, 9] cm) or desired length.

Purl 2 rounds.

Work k2tog picot BO around all sts, chaining 2 sts between each BO st.

UNDERCOLLAR

With larger 12" circ needle and A and working from wrong side of sweater, PU&K 80 (90, 90, 90, 100, 100) sts around neck opening. (Seam will be to the right side of the work so the collar folds over it.)

NEXT ROUND: Place marker to note start of round, (k5, YO); rep to end of round—96 (108, 108, 108, 120, 120) sts.

Work 5 rounds even in St st.

NEXT ROUND: (K6, YO); rep to end of round—112 (126, 126, 126, 140, 140) sts.

Work 5 rounds even in St st.

NEXT ROUND: (K7, YO); rep to end of round—128 (144, 144, 144, 160, 160) sts.

Work 5 rounds even in St st.

NEXT ROUND: (K8, YO); rep to end of round—144 (162, 162, 162, 180, 180) sts.

Work 5 rounds even in St st.

NEXT ROUND: (K9, YO); rep to end of round—160 (180, 180, 180, 200, 200) sts.

Work 2 rounds even in St st.

NEXT ROUND: (K5, YO); rep to end of round—192 (216, 216, 216, 240, 240) sts.

Work 2 rounds even in St st.

Using crochet hook, work a k2tog picot BO around all sts.

OVERCOLLAR

Return to row where Undercollar was picked up. With smaller 12" circ needle and B, pick up 1 purl bump from each st in purl round—80 (90, 90, 90, 100, 100) bumps are on needle. With B, (k1, m1) 40 (40, 40, 40, 50, 50) times—120 (130, 130, 130, 150, 150) sts. Beg Chart C (Overcollar) around all sts, placing a marker to note start of round. Work all rounds in charted pat, inc in Round 12 as directed—132 (143, 143, 143, 165, 165) sts. After Chart C is worked, work in St st until piece measures 2" (5 cm) shorter than Undercollar.

Work 2 rounds in garter st.

Using crochet hook, work a k2tog picot BO.

Above the Waist

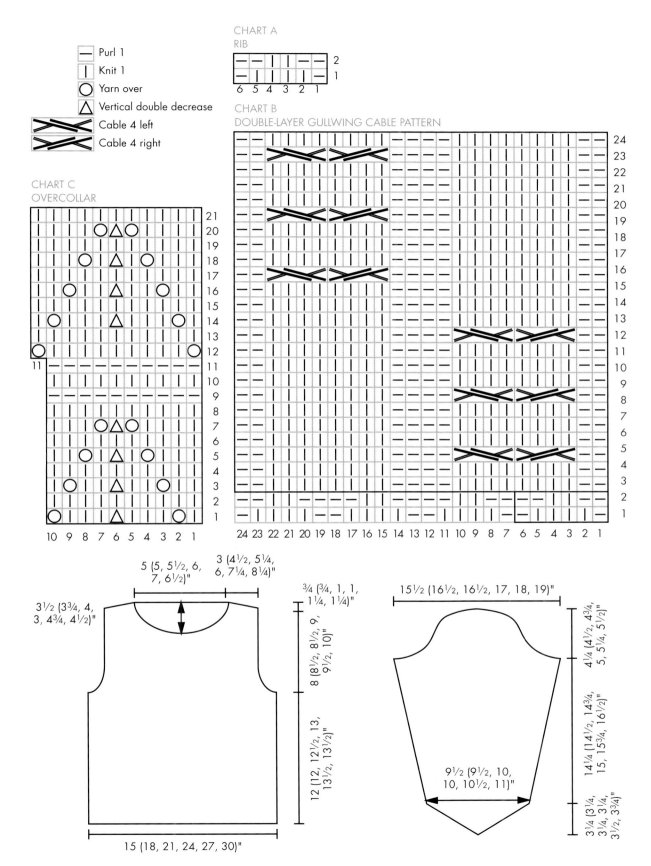

Purl 1
Knit 1
Yarn over
Vertical double decrease
Cable 4 left
Cable 4 right

CHART A
RIB

CHART B
DOUBLE-LAYER GULLWING CABLE PATTERN

CHART C
OVERCOLLAR

5 (5, 5½, 6, 7, 6½)"

3 (4½, 5¼, 6, 7¼, 8¼)"

¾ (¾, 1, 1, 1¼, 1¼)"

3½ (3¾, 4, 3, 4¾, 4½)"

8 (8½, 8½, 9, 9½, 10)"

12 (12, 12½, 13, 13½, 13½)"

15 (18, 21, 24, 27, 30)"

15½ (16½, 16½, 17, 18, 19)"

4¼ (4½, 4½, 4¾, 5, 5¼, 5½)"

14¼ (14½, 14¾, 15, 15¾, 16½)"

9½ (9½, 10, 10, 10½, 11)"

3¼ (3¼, 3¼, 3¼, 3½, 3¾)"

Dark Victory

If you thought wool couldn't be sexy, you haven't knit this tunic-length Malabrigo yoke pullover. When a wool is as soft, luxurious, and stunningly dyed as this, it *begs* to be worn close to the body! Shaping in the front and sides emphasize a womanly form, while neckline colorwork details draw attention to the face and throat.

Skill Level
INTERMEDIATE

SIZE

To fit bust: 30 (34, 38, 42, 48, 54)" (76 [86, 96.5, 106.5, 122, 137] cm)

FINISHED MEASUREMENTS

Bust: 33 (37, 41, 45, 51, 57)" (84 [94, 104, 114, 129.5, 145] cm)

Length: 24½ (25, 26¼, 27¾, 29½, 30¼)" (62 [63.5, 65.5, 70.5, 75, 77] cm)

MATERIALS

Merino Worsted by Malabrigo (3½ oz [100 g] ball, each approx 216 yds [197 m], 100% pure Merino wool)

A: Burgundy Dash 144, 4 (4, 5, 5, 6, 6) balls or 851 (918, 996, 1078, 1192, 1292) yds (776 [837, 908.5, 983, 1087, 1178.5] m) worsted weight yarn

B: Frank Ochre 35, 1 (1, 1, 1, 1, 1) ball or 106 (115, 125, 135, 149, 162) yds (96.5 [105, 114, 123, 136, 147.5] m) worsted weight yarn

C: Peach Tree 53, 1 (1, 1, 1, 1, 1) ball or 106 (115, 135, 149, 162) yds (96.5 [105, 114, 123, 136, 147.5] m) worsted weight yarn

Size 7 (4.5 mm) circular needle 36" (91 cm) long

Size 8 (5 mm) circular needle 36" (91 cm) long, or size to obtain gauge

Shorter needles may be used for yoke and neck. See Circular Stress page 112 for thoughts on circular needle lengths.

Stitch markers in yellow and blue

Darning needle

36" (91.4 cm) of ribbon to thread through yoke (optional)

GAUGE

4.25 sts and 6 rows = 1" (2.5 cm) over St st using larger needle

Refer to glossary on page 136 for: K2togR, K2togL, Twisted Float Left Slant, Twisted Float Right Slant, St st, YO.

BODY

With smaller needle and A, cast on 144 (160, 176, 192, 216, 240) sts. Join, placing marker to note start of round.

Work in k2, p2 rib for 2 rounds, inc 2 sts in last round of ribbing—146 (162, 178, 194, 218, 242) sts.

Change to larger needles.

ESTABLISH SLIP STITCH COLORWORK PATTERN (CHART A)

EST RIB: With A, k1, *p2, k2, repeat from * over next 36 (40, 44, 48, 56, 60) sts, end k1, place yellow marker (pym), k35 (39, 43, 47, 51, 59) sts, pym, k1, (p2, k2) over next 36 (40, 44, 48, 56, 60) sts, end k1, place blue marker (pbm), k35 (39, 43, 47, 51, 59) sts to end of round.

ROUNDS 1 AND 3: With A, work in rib to ym, sm, k1, (sl 1, p1); rep to 1 st before next ym, k1, sm, work in rib to next marker, sm, k1, (s1, p1); rep to 1 st before end of round, end k1.

ROUNDS 2 AND 4: With B, work in rib as est and work in St st between yellow markers over slipped stitch sections.

Rep last 4 rounds until piece measures 3¾ (3¾, 4, 4, 4¼, 4½)" (9.5 [9.5, 10, 10, 11, 11.5] cm) from caston. Tip: The yellow markers note the edges of the center front panel; the dec for hip and inc for bust happen on either side of the yellow markers. The blue markers note the edges of the center back panel; the dec for hip shaping happens on either side of blue markers.

HIP SHAPING

NEXT ROUND: Cont in pats as est with A only, (work in rib to marker, sm, k2togL, work in pat to 2 sts before next marker, k2togR, sm) twice, dec of 4 sts—140 (156, 172, 188, 212, 236) sts.

Cont in pat as est and always working sts on either side of marker as knit sts, work 3 rounds even with no shaping. Rep last 4 rounds until 124 (140, 156, 176, 200, 224) sts rem.

WAIST SHAPING

Work even with no shaping until piece measures 11¾ (11¾, 12½, 13, 13¾, 14)" (30 [30, 32, 33, 35, 35.5] cm) from cast-on.

BUST SHAPING

NEXT ROUND: Cont in pat as est, work in rib to yellow marker, sm, inc 1, work in pat to next yellow marker, inc 1 st, sm, work rem sts in pats as est, inc of 2 sts—126 (142, 158, 178, 202, 226) sts.

NEXT ROUND: Cont in pat as est, always working sts on either side of marker as knit sts.

Rep last 2 rounds until there are 144 (160, 176, 192, 216, 240) sts. *At the same time,* when piece measures 19¾ (19¾, 21, 22, 23¼, 23½)" (50 [50, 53.5, 56, 59, 59.5] cm) from cast-on, divide Front and Back as follows.

DIVIDE FOR FRONT AND BACK

NEXT ROUND: *Work 15 (17, 19, 21, 23, 27) sts in rib as est, BO 6 sts, work 15 (17, 19, 21, 23, 27) sts to next marker, work in pat as est to next marker. Rep from * once more.

Set aside rem 60 (68, 76, 84, 96, 108) sts at Front and Back to work later.

SLEEVES (MAKE 2)

Sleeves are worked back and forth.

With smaller needle and A, cast on 34 (34, 34, 38, 38, 42) sts.

ROW 1 (RS): K1, (p2, k2); rep to last st, end k1.

Change to larger needles and work in rib as est, k4, inc 1, pm, work to last 4 sts, pm, inc 1, work to end of row.

NEXT ROW (WS): Work in rib as est.

NEXT ROW (RS): Work to marker, inc 1 st, sm, work to next marker in rib as est, sm, inc 1 st, work to end of row.

Cont in this manner, inc 1 st each edge every 4 rows a total of 22 (23, 24, 24, 26, 25) times, incorporating new sts into rib—78 (80, 82, 86, 90, 92) sts.

Work even until piece measures 16¼ (16½, 16¾, 17, 17½, 18)" (41.5 [42, 42.9, 43.6, 44.9, 46.2] cm) from cast-on.

BO 6 sts at start of next 2 rows—66 (68, 70, 74, 78, 80) sts rem.

JOINING ROUND

SLIP ALL PIECES ONTO ONE NEEDLE: 60 (68, 76, 84, 96, 108) Front sts, 66 (68, 70, 74, 78, 80) right Sleeve sts, 60 (68, 76, 84, 96, 108) Back sts, 66 (68, 70, 74, 78, 80) left Sleeve sts—252 (272, 292, 316, 348, 376) sts total for Yoke.

YOKE

NEXT ROUND: With A, knit, inc 4 (0, 4, 4, 4, 0) sts evenly around work—256 (272, 296, 320, 352, 376) sts.

NEXT ROUND: Knit, placing a marker every 32 (34, 37, 40, 44, 47) sts and a contrasting marker to note start of round—8 markers total.

NEXT ROUND: Purl all sts, dec 1 st between each set of markers—248 (264, 288, 312, 344, 368) sts.

NEXT ROUND: With C, knit.

NEXT ROUND: Purl.

Rep last 4 rounds—240 (256, 280, 304, 336, 360) sts.

BEGIN TWISTED FLOAT BAND (CHART B)

NEXT ROUND (WS): Turn work so WS is facing. With A and B, work Twisted Float Right Slant around all sts.

Note: Strands from the balls of yarn will twist.

NEXT ROUND (WS): Continuing on the WS, work Twisted Float Left Slant.

Note: This will untwist the strands of yarn.

Rep last 2 rounds once, then with A and C rep last 2 rounds twice more (8 rounds total). At end of last round, turn piece so that RS is facing as you work.

Change to smaller needles and with A, knit 1 round, then purl 1 round.

NEXT ROUND: (K4, p4); rep 30 (32, 35, 38, 42, 45) times to end of round.

Work in k4, p4 rib for 3 more rounds.

NEXT ROUND: (K4, p1, p2tog, p1); rep to end of round—210 (224, 245, 266, 294, 315) sts.

Work k4, p3 rib for 3 rounds.

NEXT ROUND: (K1, k2tog, k1, p3); rep to end of round—180 (192, 210, 228, 252, 270) sts.

Work k3, p3 rib for 3 rounds.

NEXT ROUND: (K4, p2tog, p1); rep to end of round—150 (160, 175, 190, 210, 225) sts.

Work k3, p2 rib for 3 rounds.

NEXT ROUND: (K2tog, k1, p3); rep to end of round—120 (128, 140, 152, 168, 180) sts.

Work k2, p2 rib for 3 rounds.

Change to C and smaller needles, cont in rib as est until Yoke measures 4¾ (5¼, 5¼, 5¾, 6¼, 6¾)" (12 [13.5, 13.5, 14.5, 16, 17] cm) from joining round. BO all sts loosely.

FINISHING

Sew underarm seams, steam-block.

Thread ribbon or several strands of yarn through YOs at Yoke if desired.

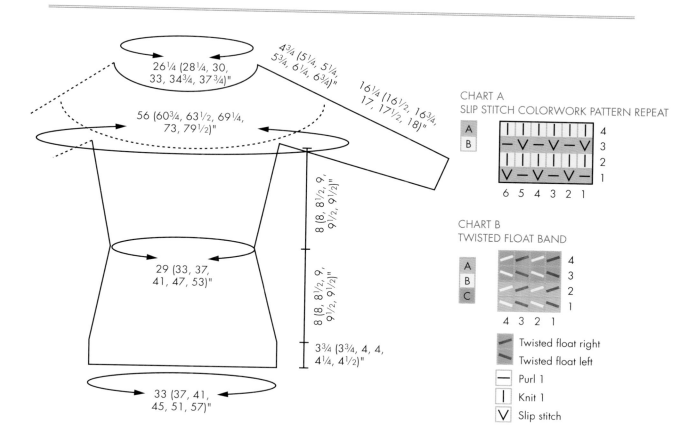

CHART A
SLIP STITCH COLORWORK PATTERN REPEAT

CHART B
TWISTED FLOAT BAND

Twisted float right
Twisted float left
Purl 1
Knit 1
Slip stitch

Below the Waist

"Awoman who goes to bed with a man ought to lay aside her modesty with her skirt, and put it on again with her petticoat."

—Michel de Montaigne, French Philosopher

We live in an amazing time in fashion history. Any length of skirt, from micromini to ankle-length ball gown, can easily reach the height of fashion. We have no strong-arm design police arbitrarily designating a set length as the "fashionable length" for this season. Free at last!

We can determine which skirt lengths and shapes look good on us. We can control the details, and we can make handknit skirts that are flattering, easy to wear, and that allow us to express ourselves with every twirl and stride. As you look through this collection of skirts and dresses, bear in mind that *you* can change lengths, make some longer or shorter, so that the design suits you. Most of the skirts have a section in the pattern that tells you to "knit until piece measures X or desired length."

See, you can make your skirt any length your little heart desires . . .

An Affair to Remember

Strong women wear strong skirts. Sexy, strong women wear sexy, strong skirts (and if they have flirty lace godets at the sides, then so much the better!). With stitch markers and counting skills, you'll find that this tulip skirt breaks down into simple bits—a tube knit with shaping, for example—and suddenly you'll be binding off the hem and looking for a Senate campaign to manage.

Skill Level
ADVANCED

SIZE

To fit hip: 30 (34, 38, 42, 48, 52)" (76 [86, 96, 106.5, 122, 132] cm)

FINISHED MEASUREMENTS

Waist: 26 (30, 34, 38, 44, 48)" (66 [76, 86, 96.5, 112, 122] cm)

Hip: 33 (37, 41, 45, 51, 55)" (84 [94, 104, 114, 129.5, 140] cm)

Length: 23½ (25, 26½, 28, 28¾, 29½)" (59.5 [63.5, 67, 71, 73, 75] cm)

MATERIALS

Amaizing by South West Trading Co. (1¾ oz [50 g] balls, each approx 143 yds (130 m), 100% corn fiber), Grenadine 366, 11 (12, 12, 13, 14, 14) balls or 620 (687, 741, 801, 875, 927) yds (565 [620, 675, 730, 798, 846] m) worsted weight yarn.

Size 8 (5 mm) circular needle at least 24" (61 cm) long, or size to obtain gauge

Size 10 (6 mm) circular needle at least 24" (61 cm) long, or size to obtain gauge

Cable needle (optional)

Stitch markers, including red and another contrasting color

1" (2.5 cm) wide elastic to fit waist plus 1" (2.5 cm)

Darning needle

Sewing needle and thread

GAUGE

4 sts and 5 rows = 1" (2.5 cm) over St st using a double strand of yarn and larger needles

Refer to glossary on page 136 for: C4L, C4R, K2togL, K2togR, St st, and YO.

WAISTBAND

With smaller needles and a single strand of A, cast on 112 (128, 144, 160, 176, 192) sts.

Work in St st for 8 rows, end with a WS row.

NEXT ROW (RS): K7 (8, 9, 10, 0, 0), (k14 [16, 18, 20, 0, 0], k2tog) 8 times, knit to end of row—104 (120, 136, 152, 176, 192) sts.

Note: 2 largest sizes are not decreased.

Change to larger needles and add a second strand of yarn. Remainder of skirt is worked with a double strand of yarn.

NEXT 2 ROWS: Knit (you are creating garter ridge).

NEXT ROW (WS): Purl.

ESTABLISH GORES

NEXT ROW (RS): K4 (8, 8, 8, 14, 14) sts [back panel], pm, p1, k4, p1 [cable], place red marker, p1 (k2, p2) 7 (7, 9, 11, 11, 13) times, k2, p1 [side panel], pm, p1, k4, p1 [left front cable], pm, k8 (16, 16, 16, 28, 28) sts [front panel], pm, p1, k4, p1 [right front cable], place red marker, p1 (k2, p2) 7 (7, 9, 11, 11, 13) times, k2, p1 [side panel], pm, p1, k4, p1 [cable], pm, k rem 4 (8, 8, 8, 14, 14) sts [Back panel]—104 (120, 136, 152, 176, 192) sts.

Join work, place contrasting marker to note center back. From this point on work in the round.

Work in rib on sides and in St st across front and back panels as est. Work 4 cables along side fronts and backs by following Chart A (Tulip Cable).

Work even in pats as est until piece measures 5¼ (5¾, 6¼, 6¾, 7, 7¼)" (13.5 [14.5, 16, 17, 18, 18.5] cm) or reaches just to widest part of hip from rev St st ridge (garter ridge). End with row 4 of Chart A.

START SIDE SHAPING

NEXT ROUND: Beg working Chart B (Tulip Side Panel) along side panels of skirt. Work traveling cables every 4 rounds in the same round as previously established cables as follows:

Work to first red marker, sm, p1, C4L, (k2, p2) 5 (5, 7, 9, 9, 11) times, C4R, p1, work to second red marker, p1, C4L, (k2, p2) 5 (5, 7, 9, 9, 11) times, C4R, p1, work to end of round.

Maintaining pats as est, work C4R and C4L within side panels every fourth row. This will move the traveling cables 2 sts closer to center of side panels every fourth row, increasing the St st area and decreasing ribbing area on side panels.

Cont working fronts and backs as est while working traveling cables at side panels in this manner until only 2 purl sts rem at center of side panel. Panel will look like this:

K4 (8, 8, 8, 14, 14) sts [back panel], sm, p1, C4L, p1, srm, p1, k14 (14, 18, 22, 22, 26) sts [back side panel], p2, k14 (14, 18, 22, 22, 26) sts, p1 [front side panel], sm, p1, C4L [left front cable], p1, sm, k8 (16, 16, 16, 28, 28) sts [front panel], sm, p1, C4L, p1 [right front cable], sm, p1, k14 (14, 18, 22, 22, 26) sts, [side front panel], p2, k14 (14, 18, 22, 22, 26) sts, p1, [side back panel], sm, p1, C4L, p1, sm, k rem 4 (8, 8, 8, 14, 14) sts, [back panel]—104 (120, 136, 152, 176, 192) sts.

START SIDE LACE

Cont front and back panels and cables as est, work side lace panel as follows:

ROUND 1: Work to first red marker, p1, k1, YO, k2togL, YO, k11 (11, 15, 19, 19, 23) sts, p2, k11 (11, 15, 19, 19, 23) sts, YO, k2togR, YO, k1, p1, work to second red marker, p1, k1, YO, k2togL, YO, k11 (11, 15, 19, 19, 23) sts, p2, k11 (11, 15, 19, 19, 23) sts, YO, k2togR, YO, k1, p1, work to end of round—108 (124, 140, 156, 180, 196) sts.

ROUND 2 AND ALL EVEN-NUMBERED ROUNDS: Work in pat as est, knitting all sts in lace sections from prev round.

ROUND 3: Work to first red marker, p1, k1, YO, (k2togL, YO) twice, k10 (10, 14, 18, 18, 22) sts, p2, k10 (10, 14, 18, 18, 22) sts, (YO, k2togR) twice, YO, k1, p1, work to second red marker, p1, k1, YO, (k2togL, YO) twice, k10 (10, 14, 18, 18, 22) sts, p2, k10 (10, 14, 18, 18, 22) sts, (YO, k2togR) twice, YO, k1, p1, work to end of round—112 (128, 144, 160, 184, 200) sts.

ROUND 5: Work to first red marker, p1, k1, YO, (k2togL, YO) 3 times, k9 (9, 13, 17, 17, 21) sts, p2, k9 (9, 13, 17, 17, 21) sts, (YO, k2togR) 3 times, YO, k1, p1, work to second red marker, p1, k1, YO, (k2togL, YO) 3 times, k9 (9, 13, 17, 17, 21) sts, p2, k9 (9, 13, 17, 17, 21) sts, (YO, k2togR) 3 times, YO, k1, p1, work to end of round—116 (132, 148, 164, 188, 204) sts.

Cont in this manner, working an additional YO/Dec at either edge of side panels as est, until the only nonlace sts in each side panel are the center p2 sts—156 (172, 204, 236, 252, 284) sts.

NEXT ODD-NUMBERED ROUND: Work to first red marker, p1, k1, (YO, k2togL) 13 (13, 17, 21, 21, 25) times, p2, (k2togR, YO) 13 (13, 17, 21, 21, 25) times, k1, p1, work to second red marker, p1, k1, (YO, k2togL) 13 (13, 17, 21, 21, 25) times, p2, (k2togR, YO) 13 (13, 17, 21, 21, 25) times, k1, p1, work to end of round—156 (172, 204, 236, 252, 284) sts.

Work even with no shaping until piece measures 22½ (24, 25½, 27, 27¾, 28½)" (57 [61, 65, 68.5, 70.5, 72] cm) from garter ridge.

Work 4 rounds of garter st, then BO all sts loosely.

FINISHING

Block piece, weave in ends. The maize fabric will want to stretch lengthwise, so don't be afraid to pull it. See Blocking with Steam, page 112, for more information on blocking. Turn waistband under and sew cast-on edge to underside of skirt. Draw elastic through waistband and tack ends of elastic together.

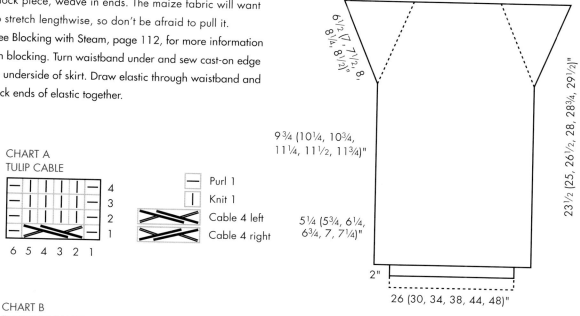

62½ (68¾, 81½, 94½, 100¾, 113½)"

6½ (7, 7½, 8,
8¾, 8½)"

9¾ (10¼, 10¾,
11¼, 11½, 11¾)"

23½ (25, 26½, 28, 28¾, 29½)"

5¼ (5¾, 6¼,
6¾, 7, 7¼)"

2"

26 (30, 34, 38, 44, 48)"

CHART A
TULIP CABLE

	4
	3
	2
	1

6 5 4 3 2 1

— Purl 1

| Knit 1

Cable 4 left

Cable 4 right

CHART B
TULIP SIDE PANEL

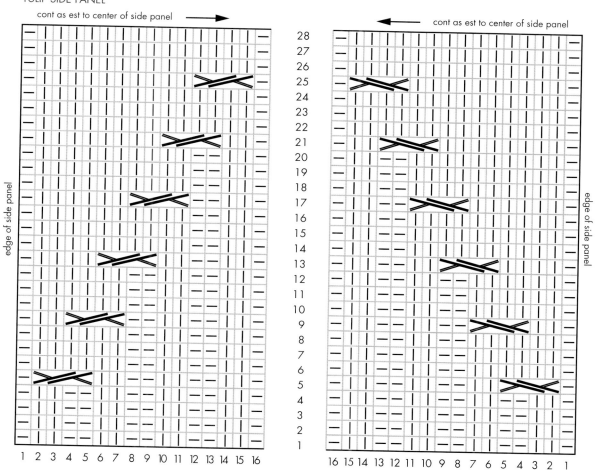

cont as est to center of side panel →

edge of side panel

1 2 3 4 5 6 7 8 9 10 11 12 13 14 15 16

28 27 26 25 24 23 22 21 20 19 18 17 16 15 14 13 12 11 10 9 8 7 6 5 4 3 2 1

← cont as est to center of side panel

edge of side panel

16 15 14 13 12 11 10 9 8 7 6 5 4 3 2 1

Now, Voyager

Imagine Autumn in Provence: the tourists have gone home, the gardens are cleared, and the evenings lengthen into deep, starlit nights. A hand-quilted matelasse comforter, fresh from an airing in the crisp afternoon sea air, is folded invitingly at the foot of the bed. This skirt is inspired by a style of French quilt stitching, with a drape and vertical grid pattern designed to flatter any figure. Machine-washable silk makes this skirt practical; decorative chain embroidery makes it memorable.

Skill Level
EASY

SIZE
To fit waist: 23 (29, 35, 39, 45, 51)" (58.5 [74, 88.5, 99, 114, 129.5] cm)

FINISHED MEASUREMENTS
Waist: 22½ (28, 33½, 39¼, 44¾, 50½)" (57 [71, 85, 99.5, 113.5, 128] cm)

Hem Circumference: 67¼ (84, 100¾, 117½, 134½, 151¼)" (171 [213, 256, 298, 342, 384] cm)

Length: 23 (26¼, 29½, 33¼, 37, 41)" (58.5 [65.5, 75, 84.5, 94, 104] cm)

MATERIALS
Passion by Yarn Source/Lambikins Hideaway (1¾ oz [50 g] skeins, each approx 150 yds [137 m], 100% silk)

A: Corn Silk 11, 5 (6, 7, 8, 9, 10) balls or 754 (893, 1032, 1149, 1296, 1446) yds (687.5 [814.5, 941, 1048, 1182, 1319] m) worsted weight yarn

B: Chocolate 13, 1 (1, 1, 1, 1, 1) ball or 94 (112, 129, 144, 162, 181) yds (85.5 [102, 117.5, 131.5, 147.5, 165] m) worsted weight yarn

C: Canyon 16, 1 (1, 1, 1, 1, 1) ball or 38 (45, 52, 57, 65, 72) yds (34.5 [41, 47.5, 52, 59.5, 65.5] m) worsted weight yarn

D: Storm 7, 1 (1, 1, 1, 1, 1) ball or 28 (33, 39, 43, 49, 54) yds (25.5 [33, 35.5, 39, 44.5, 49] m) worsted weight yarn

E: Key Lime 17, 1 (1, 1, 1, 1, 1) ball or 28 (33, 43, 49, 54) yds (25.5 [33, 35.5, 39, 44.5, 49] m) worsted weight yarn

F: Envy 19, 1 (1, 1, 1, 1, 1) ball or or 28 (33, 39, 43, 49, 54) yds (25.5 [33, 35.5, 39, 44.5, 49] m) worsted weight yarn

Size 5 (3.75 mm) 2 circular needles at least 24" (61 cm) long

Size 6 (4 mm) 2 circular needles at least 24" (61 cm) long, or size to obtain gauge

See Circular Stress page 112 for thoughts on circular needle lengths.

Size F/5 (3.75 mm) crochet hook

1" (2.5 cm) wide elastic to fit waist plus 1" (2.5 cm)

Darning needle

Sewing needle and thread

Refer to glossary on page 136 for: Sl st, WYIB. See page 29 for embroidery stitch: Decorative Chain Embroidery.

WAISTBAND

With large needles and A, cast on 112 (140, 168, 196, 224, 252) sts.

With smaller needles, k6 rounds, p1 round, k6 rounds. Change to larger needles.

BAND PATTERN

Note: After each round listed in each band, knit one plain round. The plain knit rounds are *not* listed in the sections that follow.

For skirt as shown, work to band 10 (11, 11, 12, 13, 14), or work to desired length.

BAND 1

NEXT ROUND: (K6, sl 1 st); rep to end.

Rep last 2 rounds 3 times.

NEXT ROUND: (P6, wyib sl 1); rep to end.

NEXT ROUND: (K3, m1, k3, sl 1 st); rep to end of round—128 (160, 192, 224, 256, 288) sts.

BAND 2

NEXT ROUND: (K7, sl 1 st); rep to end.

Rep last 2 rounds 4 times.

NEXT ROUND: (P7, wyib sl 1); rep to end.

NEXT ROUND: (K4, m1, k3, sl 1 st); rep to end of round—144 (180, 216, 252, 288, 324) sts.

BAND 3

NEXT ROUND: (K8, sl 1 st); rep to end.

Rep last 2 rounds 5 times.

NEXT ROUND: (K4, m1, k4, sl 1 st); rep to end of round—160 (200, 240, 280, 320, 360) sts.

BAND 4

NEXT ROUND: (K9, sl 1 st); rep to end.

Rep last 2 rounds 6 times.

NEXT ROUND: (P9, wyib sl 1); rep to end.

NEXT ROUND: (K5, m1, k4, sl 1 st); rep to end of round—176 (220, 264, 308, 352, 396) sts.

BAND 5

NEXT ROUND: (K10, sl 1 st); rep to end.

Rep last 2 rounds 7 times.

NEXT ROUND: (P10, wyib sl 1); rep to end.

Embroidery detail.

NEXT ROUND: (K5, m1, k5, sl 1 st); rep to end of round—192 (240, 288, 336, 384, 432) sts.

BAND 6

NEXT ROUND: (K11, sl 1 st); rep to end.

Rep last 2 rounds 7 times.

NEXT ROUND: (P11, wyib sl 1); rep to end.

NEXT ROUND: (K6, m1, k5, sl 1 st); rep to end of round—208 (260, 312, 364, 416, 468) sts.

BAND 7

NEXT ROUND: (K12, sl 1 st); rep to end.

Rep last 2 rounds 8 times.

NEXT ROUND: (P12, wyib sl 1); rep to end.

NEXT ROUND: (K6, m1, k6, sl 1 st); rep to end of round—224 (280, 336, 392, 448, 504) sts.

BAND 8

NEXT ROUND: (K13, sl 1 st); rep to end.

Rep last 2 rounds 9 times.

NEXT ROUND: (P13, wyib sl 1); rep to end.

NEXT ROUND: (K7, m1, k6, sl 1 st); rep to end of round—240 (300, 360, 420, 480, 540) sts.

BAND 9

NEXT ROUND: (K14, sl 1 st); rep to end.

Rep last 2 rounds 9 times.

NEXT ROUND: (P14, wyib sl 1); rep to end.

NEXT ROUND: (K7, m1, k7, sl 1 st); rep to end of round—256 (320, 384, 448, 512, 576) sts.

BAND 10

NEXT ROUND: (K15, sl 1 st); rep to end.

Rep last 2 rounds 10 times.

NEXT ROUND: (P15, wyib sl 1); rep to end.

NEXT ROUND: (K8, m1, k7, sl 1 st); rep to end of round—272 (340, 408, 476, 544, 612) sts.

BAND 11

NEXT ROUND: (K16, sl 1 st); rep to end.

Rep last 2 rounds 11 times.

NEXT ROUND: (P16, wyib sl 1); rep to end.

NEXT ROUND: (K8, m1, k8, sl 1 st); rep to end of round—288 (360, 432, 504, 576, 648) sts.

BAND 12

NEXT ROUND: (K17, sl 1 st); rep to end.

Rep last 2 rounds 11 times.

NEXT ROUND: (P17, wyib sl 1); rep to end.

NEXT ROUND: (K9, m1, k8, sl 1 st); rep to end of round—304 (380, 456, 532, 608, 684) sts.

BAND 13

NEXT ROUND: (K18, sl 1 st); rep to end.

Rep last 2 rounds 12 times.

NEXT ROUND: (P18, wyib sl 1); rep to end.

NEXT ROUND: (K9, m1, k9, sl 1 st); rep to end of round—320 (400, 480, 560, 640, 720) sts.

BAND 14

NEXT ROUND: (K19, sl 1 st); rep to end.

Rep last 2 rounds 13 times.

NEXT ROUND: (P19, wyib sl 1); rep to end.

NEXT ROUND: (K10, m1, k9, sl 1 st); rep to end of round—336 (420, 504, 588, 672, 756) sts.

HEM

NEXT ROUND: (K2tog, YO); rep to end of round.

NEXT ROUND: Switch to smaller needle and knit.

Cont with smaller needle, rep last round 3 more times.

Loosely BO all sts with larger needle.

FINISHING

Steam-block piece. Turn hem under at eyelet round and stitch to underside of skirt. Turn Waistband facing under at purl round and stitch in place, leaving 1" (2.5 cm) opening to thread elastic through.

Measure a piece of elastic 1" (2.5 cm) larger than waist measurement and draw through Waistband casing. Stitch ends in place, then, using sewing needle and thread, sew rem 1" (2.5 cm) of casing closed.

EMBROIDERY

Following chain-stitch embroidery chart, work embroidery around skirt bottom. Work as much or as little embroidery as you choose, working one color at a time around entire circumference of skirt.

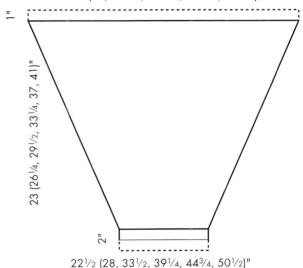

67¼ (84, 100¾, 117½, 134½, 151¼)"

1"

23 (26¼, 29½, 33¼, 37, 41)"

2"

22½ (28, 33½, 39¼, 44¾, 50½)"

CHAIN STITCH EMBROIDERY CHART

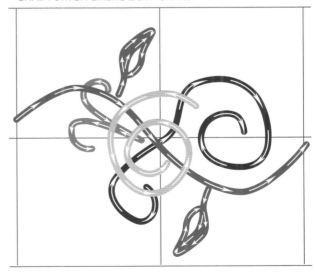

West Side Story

My older cousins visited from Virginia in 1965 and brought the original cast album of *West Side Story* with them. They were sophisticated, they wore lipstick and bras, and, to my five-year-old eyes, there were no more beautiful girls in the world. Some things never leave you, and the frisson of excitement I felt every time I lost myself in the photos on the album cover they left behind made me feel glamorous beyond my years. This skirt is my own personal homage to Anita—flirtation through the eyes of a child in Toledo, Ohio.

Skill Level
EASY

SIZE
To fit waist: 22 (26, 32, 36, 39, 48)" (56.4 [66, 79, 89, 99, 121.9] cm)

FINISHED MEASUREMENTS
Waist: 22 (26, 31, 35, 39, 48)" (56.4 [66, 81, 91, 101.5, 117] cm)

Length: 16½ (19, 21½, 24, 25¼, 26½)" (42 [48.7, 54.5, 61, 64, 67] cm)

MATERIALS
A: Star by Classic Elite (1¾ oz [50 g] skeins, each approx 112 yds [102 m], 99% cotton, 1% lycra), Indian Paintbrush 5155, 3 (3, 4, 4, 5, 5) skeins or 331 (379, 444, 488, 526, 579) yds (302 [345.5, 401.5, 445, 479.5, 528] m) sportweight, nubby, stretchy yarn

B: Potpourri by Classic Elite (1¾ oz [50 g] skeins, each approx 86 yds [78 m], 100% nylon ribbon), Antique Orange 7285, 2 (3, 3, 4, 4, 4) skeins or 206 (235, 273, 303, 326, 359) yds (188 [214.5, 249, 276.5, 297.5, 327.5] m) bulky ribbon yarn

C: Potpourri by Classic Elite, Sunset Red 7258, 2 (3, 3, 4, 4, 4) skeins or 206 (235, 273, 303, 326, 359) yds (188 [214.5, 249, 303, 326, 359] yds (188 [214.5, 249, 276.5, 297.5, 327.5] m) bulky ribbon yarn

Size 6 (4 mm) circular needle at least 20" (51 cm) long

Size 7 (4.5 mm) circular needle at least 20" (51 cm) long, or size to obtain gauge

Size 9 (5.5 mm) circular needle at least 20" (51 cm) long

½" (1 cm) wide elastic, to fit around waist plus 2" (5 cm)

Darning needle

Sewing needle and thread

GAUGE
5.5 sts and 7 rows = 1" (2.5 cm) over k2, p2 rib using larger needle and A

Refer to glossary on page 136 for: K2, P2 Rib, PU&K, St st, YO, and YYK.

WAISTBAND FACING
With smallest needles and A, cast on 120 (144, 168, 192, 216, 264) sts.

Work in St st for 1" (2.5 cm) for all sizes, end with a RS (knit) row.

NEXT 2 ROWS: Switch to medium needles and knit (you are creating garter ridge).

Join, and from this point forward work in the round.

Work in k2, p2 rib for 6½ (7, 7½, 8, 8¼, 8½)" (16.5 [18, 19, 20.5, 21, 21.5] cm).

Stitches in garter rows of ribbon are picked up to create ruffles.

RUFFLES

RED RUFFLE PLACEMENT

Note: Do not cut A while knitting ridges for ruffle placement in other colors.

NEXT ROUND: With B, knit

NEXT ROUND: With B, purl.

Cut B. Return to A, and, working in St st (knit every round), work to 2½ (3, 3½, 4, 4¼, 4½)" (6.5 [7.5, 9, 10, 11, 11.5] cm) from B purl ridge.

ORANGE RUFFLE PLACEMENT

NEXT ROUND: With C, knit.

NEXT ROUND: With C, purl.

Cut C. Return to A, and, working in St st (knit every round), work to 2½ (3, 3½, 4, 4¼, 4½)" (6.4 [7.7, 9, 10.3, 10.9, 11.5] cm) from B purl ridge.

RED RUFFLE PLACEMENT

NEXT ROUND: With B, knit.

NEXT ROUND: With B, purl.

Cut B. Return to A, and, working in St st (knit every

round), work to 2½ (3, 3½, 4, 4¼, 4½)" (6.4 [7.7, 9, 10.3, 10.9, 11.5] cm) from B purl ridge.

ORANGE RUFFLE HEM

NEXT ROUND: With largest needle and C, knit.

NEXT ROUND: *K2, YO; rep from * to end of round 60 (72, 84, 96, 108, 132) times—180 (216, 252, 288, 324, 396) sts.

NEXT ROUND: Knit each st, wrapping yarn twice around needle for every st (YYK).

NEXT ROUND: Knit, working in the first loop in each stitch and dropping the second wrap to create an extra-long stitch.

Rep last 2 rounds once more, then work in St st if necessary until ruffle measures at least 2½ (3, 3½, 4, 4¼, 4½)" (6.5 [7.5, 9, 10, 11, 11.5] cm).

Purl 1 round.

BO all sts loosely.

RUFFLES (MAKE 3, ONE FOR EACH RIBBON STRIPE KNIT INTO SKIRT)

Working on right side of work, insert needle into each purl bump in designated ribbon stripe—120 (144, 168, 192, 216, 264) sts on needle.

Working with the same color as ribbon stripe, work ruffle as follows.

3RD RUFFLE FROM TOP

PU sts as directed above.

NEXT ROUND: With largest needle and B, knit.

NEXT ROUND: *K3, YO, rep from * to end of round 40 (48, 56, 64, 72, 88) times—160 (192, 224, 256, 288, 352) sts.

NEXT ROUND: YYK each st.

NEXT ROUND: Knit, working in the first loop in each stitch and dropping the second wrap to create an extra-long stitch.

Rep last 2 rounds once, then work in St st if necessary until ruffle measures at least 2½ (3, 3½, 4, 4¼, 4½)" (6.5 [7.5, 9, 10, 11, 11.5] cm).

Purl 1 round.

BO all sts loosely.

2ND RUFFLE FROM TOP

PU sts as directed on page 74.

NEXT ROUND: With largest needle and C, knit.

NEXT ROUND: (K4, YO); rep to end of round 30 (36, 42, 48, 54, 66) times—150 (180, 210, 240, 270, 330) sts.

NEXT ROUND: YYK each st.

NEXT ROUND: Knit, working in the first loop in each stitch and dropping the second wrap to create an extra-long stitch.

Rep last 2 rounds once, then work in St st if necessary until ruffle measures at least 2½ (3, 3½, 4, 4¼, 4½)" (6.5 [7.5, 9, 10, 11, 11.5] cm).

Purl 1 round.

BO all sts loosely.

TOP RUFFLE

PU sts as directed above.

NEXT ROUND: With largest needle and B, knit.

NEXT ROUND: (K6, YO); rep to end of round 20 (24, 28, 32, 36, 44) times—140 (168, 196, 224, 252, 308) sts.

NEXT ROUND: YYK each st.

NEXT ROUND: Knit, working in the first loop in each stitch and dropping the second wrap to create an extra-long stitch.

Rep last 2 rounds once, then work in St st if necessary until ruffle measures at least 2½ (3, 3½, 4, 4¼, 4½)" (6.5 [7.5, 9, 10, 11, 11.5] cm). Purl 1 round, BO all sts loosely.

FINISHING

Fold Waistband in half and sew to underside of Waistband, leaving a 2" (5 cm) opening. Measure the elastic around your waist and add 2" (5 cm). Thread elastic through Waistband, allowing it to overlap 1" (2.5 cm), and sew elastic together. Sew opening in Waistband.

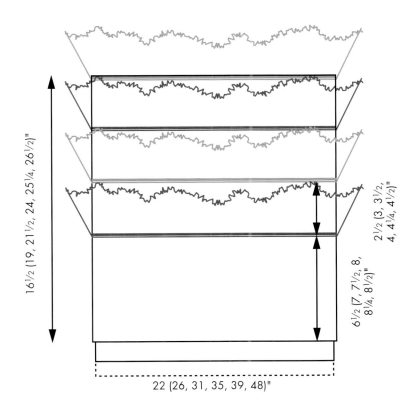

16½ (19, 21½, 24, 25¼, 26½)"

2½ (3, 3½, 4, 4¼, 4½)"

6½ (7, 7½, 8, 8¼, 8½)"

22 (26, 31, 35, 39, 48)"

All About Eve

A symphony of short-row shaping gives this skirt a drape that flatters and is easy to wear. The edges of the skirt are shaped to fold over each other, creating an interesting line and preventing unwanted flip-ups (nothing romantic about *them*!). Dupioni ribbon fabric, cut into strips and knit loosely, worked with double yarn overs in the lower area of the skirt, yields a garment that retains a handknit feeling without being too heavy or cluttered.

Skill Level
EASY

SIZE

To fit waist: 22 (26, 32, 36, 40, 46)" (56 [66, 81, 91, 101.5, 117] cm)

FINISHED MEASUREMENTS

Waist (wrapped): 22 (26, 32, 36, 40, 46)" (56 [66, 81, 91, 101.5, 117] cm)

Waist (open, excluding ties): 32 (39, 49¾, 53¼, 60½, 67½)" (81 [99, 126.5, 135, 154, 172] cm)

Length: 25¼ (26¼, 27¼, 28¼, 28¾, 29¼)" (64 [66.5, 69.5, 71.5, 73, 74.5] cm)

MATERIALS

Silk Gelato by Lantern Moon (1¾ oz [50 g] skeins, each approx 72 yds [66m], 100% silk fabric ribbon)

A: Bittersweet, 5 (6, 6, 7, 7, 8) skeins or 381 (417, 465, 501, 532, 578) yds (347.5 [380.5, 424, 457, 485, 527] m) bulky ribbon yarn

B: Raspberry, 1 (1, 1, 1, 1, 1) skein or 67 (74, 82, 88, 94, 102) yds (61 [67.5, 75, 80.5, 85.5, 93] m) bulky ribbon yarn

Size 17 (12.75 mm) circular needle at least 24" (61 cm) long and double-pointed needles, or size to obtain gauge

Stitch markers

Steam iron

Darning needle

GAUGE

2.25 sts and 2.75 rows = 1" (2.5 mm) in St st

2.25 sts and 1.5 rows = 1" (2.5 mm) in double YYK St st

Refer to glossary on page 136 for: I-Cord Cast-On, M1, St st, W&T, and YYK.

WAISTBAND AND TIES

With A and double-pointed needles, cast on 3 sts.

Create a piece of I-cord 6½ (7¾, 9½, 10¾, 12, 13¾)" (16.7 [19.9, 24.4, 27.6, 30.8, 35.3] cm) long. Cont with est cord, begin working I-cord cast-on using circular needle until 72 (88, 112, 120, 136, 152) sts have been cast on.

Leaving cast-on sts on circular needle, cont working I-cord alone using double-pointed needles until tail of I-cord length measures 16 (18, 21, 26, 37, 34)" (40.5 [45.5, 53.5, 66, 94, 86] cm).

BO and cut A.

SKIRT YOKE

ROW 1 (RS): Working with I-cord cast-on sts, slip 36 (44, 56, 60, 68, 76) sts, place marker to note center of Skirt, join B and k5 (6, 8, 9, 10, 11) sts, W&T.

NEXT ROW (WS): Purl to 5 (6, 8, 9, 10, 11) sts past center marker, W&T.

NEXT ROW: Cont in St st, work to last wrapped st, k5 (6, 8, 9, 10, 11) sts, W&T.

Rep last row until 32 (38, 50, 52, 60, 66) sts total have been worked in B—12 (14, 14, 14, 16, 16) rows total worked.

NEXT ROW: Cont in St st, work to last wrapped st, k4 (4, 6, 6, 7, 8) sts, W&T.

Rep last row until 54 (64, 84, 88, 100, 112) sts total have been worked in B—18 (21, 21, 21, 24, 24) rows total worked.

NEXT ROW: Cont in St st, work to last wrapped st, k1 (1, 2, 2, 2, 3) sts, W&T.

Rep last row until 62 (72, 96, 100, 114, 128) total have been worked in B—6 (7, 7, 7, 8, 8) rows total worked.

NEXT ROW: Cont in St st, work to last wrapped st, k2 (3, 3, 3, 4, 4) sts, W&T.

Rep last row until all sts have been worked in B, end with a WS row, remove center marker—72 (88, 112, 120, 136, 152) sts.

GORED PANEL SECTIONS

Switch to A, do not cut B.

NEXT ROW (RS): Knit.

NEXT ROW (WS): K5 (6, 7, 8, 9, 10), *pm, k9 (11, 14, 15, 17, 19); rep from * 7 times, knit rem 4 (5, 7, 7, 8, 9) sts.

YYK PATTERN SECTION

Switch to B, cut A.

ROW 1 (RS): Wrapping each st twice around needle when making knit st or m1, (knit to 1 st before marker, m1, k1, sm); rep to last marker, knit to end of row—79 (95, 119, 127, 143, 159) sts.

ROW 2 (AND ALL WS ROWS): Working only the first loop in each stitch and dropping the second wrap to create an extra-long stitch, k2, purl to last 2 sts, k2.

ROW 3: Wrapping each st twice around needle when making knit st, knit all sts.

ROWS 4–6: Rep Rows 2 and 3 once, then rep Row 2 once more.

ROW 7 (RS): (Knit to 1 st after marker, m1, k1, sm); rep to last post-marker, m1, knit to end of row—86 (102, 126, 134, 150, 166) sts.

ROWS 8–12: Rep Rows 2 and 3 twice, then rep Row 2 again.

Rep Rows 1–12 until there are a total of 100 (116, 140, 148, 164, 180) sts on needle.

Work even until skirt length measures 25¼ (26¼, 27¼, 28¼, 28¾, 29¼)" (64 [66.5, 69.5, 71.5, 73, 74.5] cm) or desired length at center point. (See Finishing.) With A, work 2 rows of garter st.

BO all sts loosely.

FINISHING

If desired, block heavily with steam and an iron as you work to determine finished, blocked length. See Blocking with Steam, page 112, for more information on blocking. The fabric will stretch quite a bit when blocked with a firm hand. Be firm to compel the fabric to relax.

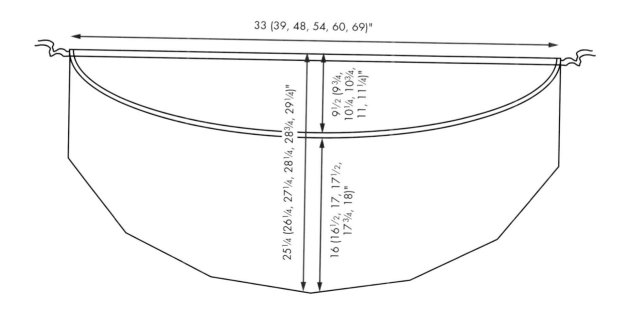

The Bishop's Wife

Afternoon tea at the Vicars, an exhibition at a Chelsea gallery, or a matinee of the new Shaw play—you'll swear you've drifted into a Dorothy Sayers novel in 1930s London when wearing this vintage-styled shirtwaist dress. The dress is knit from the waist up through the bodice, then the skirt is picked up and finished at the end—allowing you to make the skirt any length you choose! Machine-washable Merino wool blended with linen gives the fabric a magnificent drape, which snaps back into shape after washing.

Skill Level
ADVANCED

SIZE
To fit bust: 28 (30, 32, 36, 40, 44, 48, 52)" (71 [76, 82, 91, 101.5, 112, 122, 132] cm)

FINISHED MEASUREMENTS
Waist: 24 (26½, 28, 32, 36, 40, 44, 48)" (61 [68, 71, 81, 91, 101.5, 112, 122] cm)

Bust: 34½ (36, 38½, 42½, 46½, 50½, 54½, 58½)" (88 [91, 98, 108, 118, 129, 138, 149] cm)

Length: 49 (50½, 50½, 52, 52½, 54¼, 57¼, 60½)" (124.5 [129, 129, 132, 133, 137, 145.5, 154] cm)

MATERIALS
MerLin Tristan by Louet (3½ oz [100 g] skeins, each approx 250 yds [228 m], 70% Merino, 30% linen), Lilac, 12 (12, 12, 13, 13, 13, 14, 14) balls or 1655 (1723, 1771, 1892, 2002, 2122, 2257, 2400) yds (1510 [1571, 1614, 1725, 1824, 1935, 2058, 2632] m) sportweight yarn

Size 5 (3.75 mm), 2 circular needles

Size 6 (4 mm), 2 circular needles, or size to obtain gauge

See Circular Stress page 112 for thoughts on circular needle lengths.

Size F/5 (3.75 mm) crochet hook

One ¼" (6 mm) button

Darning needle

GAUGE
Blouse and Skirt: 5 sts and 8 rows = 1" (2.5 cm) over St st on larger needles

Ribbed Waist: 6 sts and 8.25 rows = 1" (2.5 cm) over k2, p2 ribbing on smaller needles (slightly stretched)

Refer to glossary on page 136 for: Garter st, K2, P2 Rib, K2togL, K2togR, M1, Provisional Cast-On, and YO.

See page 47 for crochet technique: HDC, SC.

BLOUSE

With smaller circ needles and using a provisional cast-on, CO 144 (160, 168, 192, 216, 240, 264, 288) sts. Join to work in the round. Place marker to note start of round, this will be the right side of the garment, beneath the right sleeve.

Work in k2, p2 rib for 5¾ (5¾, 6, 6, 6¼, 6¼, 6½, 6½)" (14.5 [14.5, 15, 15, 16, 16, 16.5, 16.5] cm).

Crochet collar and button detail.

NEXT ROUND: Switch to larger needles, k8 (8, 0, 0, 4, 0, 0, 0) sts, *k4 (6, 7, 8, 13, 15, 33, 36) sts, m1, rep from * 32 (24, 24, 24, 16, 16, 8, 8) times, k8 (8, 0, 0, 4, 0, 0, 0) sts—176 (184, 192, 216, 232, 256, 272, 296) sts. Work 4 rounds in garter st, then knit 1 round.

Beg with stitch 1 of the Bias Panels Chart designated for your size, rep chart 8 times around all sts.

Cont working in charted pat as est until piece measures 5¼ (5¾, 5½, 6, 6, 6½, 7½, 8¾)" (13.5 [14.7, 14.1, 15.4, 15.4, 16.7, 19.2, 22.4] cm) from start of garter st. End with a WS row.

DIVIDE FOR FRONT AND BACK

NEXT ROW (RS): Cont in pat as est, work 88 (92, 96, 108, 116, 128, 136, 148) sts. Place these Front sts on a holder or spare needle to work later.

BACK

Cont with next 88 (92, 96, 108, 116, 128, 136, 148) Back sts, working back and forth from this point on, cont as follows:

BO 4 (4, 4, 4, 6, 6, 6, 6) sts at beg of next 2 rows, then BO 2 (2, 3, 3, 3, 3, 4, 4) sts at each armhole edge twice—72 (76, 76, 88, 92, 104, 108, 120) sts rem.

Note: In the armhole shaping rows, be sure to work the inc and dec sts in the pattern nearest each armhole edge simply as knit sts. This will keep the stitch count correct for your size.

Cont working with back sts in pat as est until armhole measures 6 (6½, 6½, 7, 7, 7½, 8, 8½)" (15 [16.5, 16.5, 18, 18, 19, 20.5, 21.5] cm). End with a WS row.

NEXT ROW (RS): Work 36 (38, 38, 44, 46, 52, 54, 60) sts, join second ball of yarn and work in pat as est to end of row.

Working both sides of Back at once with separate balls of yarn, work even until armhole measures 8 (8½, 8½, 9, 9, 9½, 10, 10½)" (20.5 [21.5, 21.5, 23, 23, 24, 25.5, 26.5] cm). End with a WS row.

SHOULDER SHAPING

BO 8 (10, 9, 9, 11, 11, 12, 12) sts at each armhole edge once, then BO 8 (8, 8, 10, 10, 12, 12, 14) sts at each armhole edge twice.

BO rem 12 (12, 13, 15, 15, 17, 18, 20) sts.

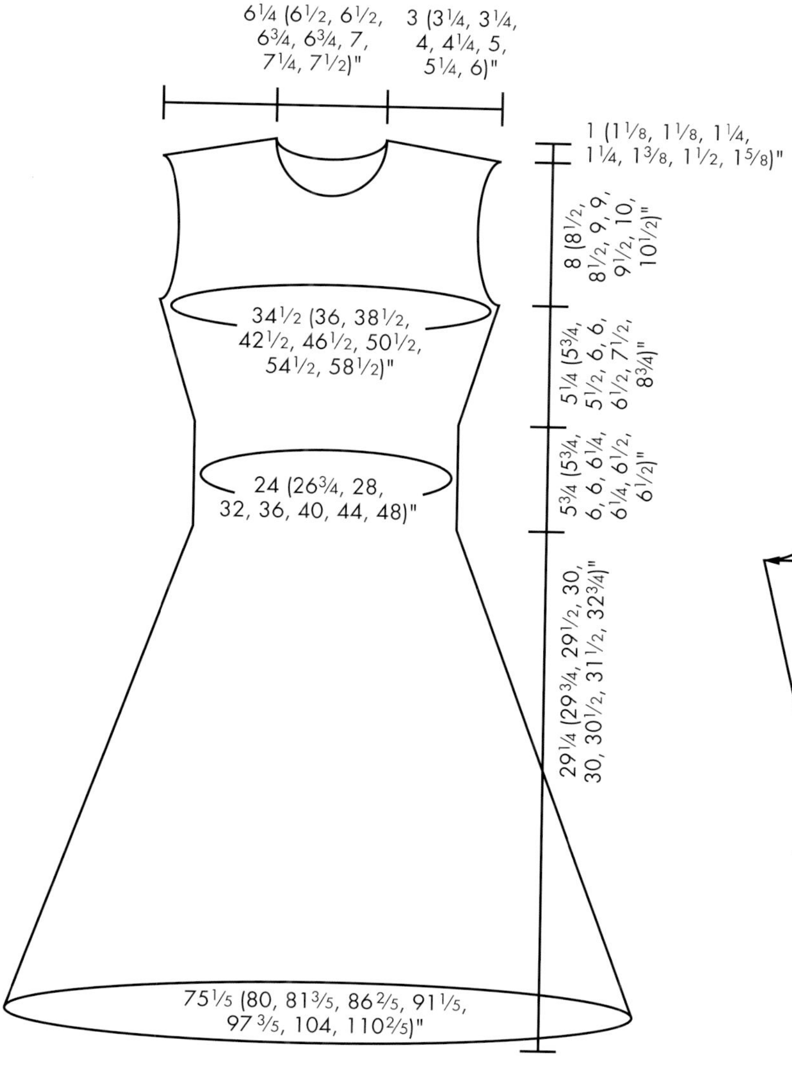

6¼ (6½, 6½, 6¾, 6¾, 7, 7¼, 7½)"
3 (3¼, 3¼, 4, 4¼, 5, 5¼, 6)"
1 (1⅛, 1⅛, 1¼, 1¼, 1⅜, 1½, 1⅝)"
8 (8½, 8½, 9, 9, 9½, 10, 10½)"
34½ (36, 38½, 42½, 46½, 50½, 54½, 58½)"
5¼ (5¾, 5½, 6, 6, 6½, 7½, 8¾)"
24 (26¾, 28, 32, 36, 40, 44, 48)"
5¾ (5¾, 6, 6, 6¼, 6¼, 6½, 6½)"
29¼ (29¾, 29½, 30, 30, 30½, 31½, 32¾)"
75⅕ (80, 81⅗, 86⅖, 91⅕, 97⅗, 104, 110⅖)"

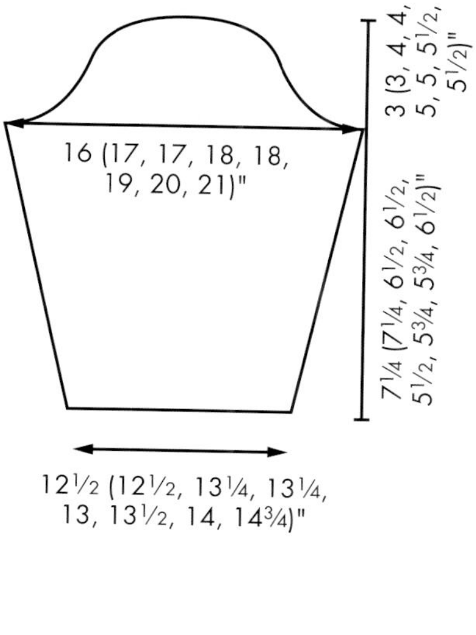

3 (3, 4, 4, 5, 5, 5½, 5½)"
16 (17, 17, 18, 18, 19, 20, 21)"
7¼ (7¼, 6½, 6½, 5½, 5¾, 5¾, 6½)"
12½ (12½, 13¼, 13¼, 13, 13½, 14, 14¾)"

FRONT

Return reserved 88 (92, 96, 108, 116, 128, 136, 148)
Front sts to needle and beg with wrong-side row, work
armhole shaping as for Back—72 (76, 76, 88, 92, 104,
108, 120) sts rem.

Work even until armhole measures 5 (5³⁄₈, 5³⁄₈, 5³⁄₄,
5³⁄₄, 6¹⁄₈, 6¹⁄₂, 6⁷⁄₈)" (12.5 [13.5, 13.5, 14.5, 14.5,
15.5, 16.5, 17.5] cm).

NECK SHAPING

Work across 32 (34, 33, 39, 40, 46, 47, 53) sts in pat
as est, BO center 8 (8, 10, 10, 12, 12, 14, 14) sts,
work rem 32 (34, 33, 39, 40, 46, 47, 53) sts in pat to
end of row. Working both sides *at the same time* with
separate balls of yarn, BO 2 (2, 2, 2, 2, 3, 3, 3) sts at
Neck edge every row twice.

BO 2 (2, 2, 2, 1, 3, 1, 1) sts at each Neck edge once,
then BO 1 (1, 1, 2, 2, 2, 2, 3) times—24 (26, 25, 29,
31, 35, 36, 40) sts rem for each Shoulder.

When Front measures same as Back to Shoulder, work
shaping as for Back.

SLEEVES

With smaller needles, cast on 62 (62, 66, 66, 66, 70,
70, 70) sts.

Work in k2, p2 ribbing for 1" (2.5 cm). End with a
WS row.

With larger needles beg working in St st and *at the same
time* inc 1 st each edge every 8 (6, 6, 4, 4, 4, 4, 4)
rows 9 (12, 10, 12, 12, 13, 15, 18) times—80 (86, 86,
90, 90, 96, 100, 106) sts.

Work even until piece measures 7¹⁄₄ (7¹⁄₄, 6¹⁄₂, 6¹⁄₂,
5¹⁄₂, 5³⁄₄, 5³⁄₄, 6¹⁄₂)" (18.5 [18.5, 16.5, 16.5, 14,
14.5, 14.5, 16.5] cm) from cast-on. End with a WS row.

CAP SHAPING

BO 10 (11, 10, 12, 12, 11, 12, 11) sts at beg of next 2
rows, BO 4 sts at beg of next 2 rows, work 2 rows even,
BO 2 sts at beg of every other row 4 times, BO 6 (6, 6,
6, 7, 7, 8, 8) sts at beg of each row 2 (2, 2, 2, 2, 4, 4,
4) times.

BO rem 24 (28, 30, 30, 28, 29, 22, 20) sts.

SKIRT

With a circ needle, pick up the provisional cast-on sts—
144 (160, 168, 192, 216, 240, 264, 288) sts.

Starting at point where original marker was placed at
right side of blouse, k9 (10, 10, 12, 13, 15, 16, 18) sts,
place marker, *k18 (20, 21, 24, 27, 30, 33, 36) sts,
place marker, rep from * to end of round, end k9 (10,
11, 12, 14, 15, 17, 18) sts.

You now have 8 sections, each with 18 (20, 21, 24, 27,
30, 33, 36) sts.

NEXT ROUND: *Work to 1 st before marker, YO, k1, sm,
k1, YO, rep from * to end of round (2 YOs per
section)—20 (22, 23, 26, 29, 32, 35, 38) sts in each
section, 160 (176, 184, 208, 232, 256, 280, 304) sts
total on needle.

NEXT 7 ROUNDS: Knit all sts.

Rep last 8 rounds, inc 2 sts in each section every eighth
round until there are a total of 48 (50, 52, 54, 58, 62,
66, 70) sts each section and 384 (400, 416, 432, 464,
496, 528, 560) sts on needle.

Work even until skirt is desired length.

NEXT ROUND: (P2tog, YO); rep to end of round.

NEXT 6 ROUNDS: Knit.

BO all sts loosely.

BELT

With crochet hook and a single strand of yarn, ch 150.

NEXT ROW: Half double crochet (hdc) into second ch from hook, hdc each ch.

NEXT 2 ROWS: Chain 2, hdc each st. Fasten off.

LEFT COLLAR

Starting at left center Back, with crochet hook and single strand of yarn, single crochet 32 (32, 32, 34, 34, 36, 36, 38) sts around to center Front of Neck opening, turn work.

NEXT ROW (WS): Ch 1, 1 SC each st—32 (32, 32, 34, 34, 36, 36, 38) sts, turn.

NEXT ROW (RS): Ch 2, hdc to last 4 sts, sc 3, sl last st, turn.

NEXT ROW (WS): Sl 3, sc 3, hdc to last st, turn.

NEXT ROW (RS): Ch 2, hdc to last 6 sts, sl 6.

Fasten off.

Rep for Right Collar, reversing shaping.

BUTTON LOOP

With crochet hook, join yarn at tip of back right Neck opening. Chain 30, single crochet into same space as join. SC down back right Neck opening edge and back up left Neck opening edge. Fasten off.

Sew button to left edge to correspond to button loop.

FINISHING

Steam-block all pieces. Sew underarm seam and baste Sleeves into armholes. Sew Sleeves in place, and, if desired, create crochet chain belt loops around waist of dress. Weave in ends.

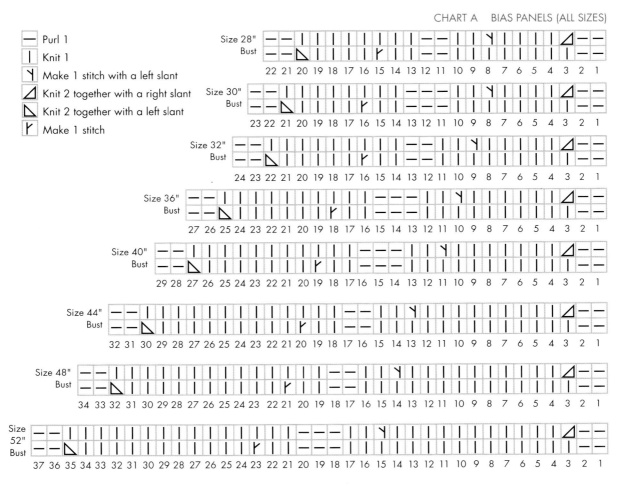

CHART A   BIAS PANELS (ALL SIZES)

Key:
— Purl 1
| Knit 1
Y Make 1 stitch with a left slant
◿ Knit 2 together with a right slant
◺ Knit 2 together with a left slant
Ɏ Make 1 stitch

Cleopatra

Leave the gold to Tutankhamen—I'd rather have the exquisite pulled linen fabrics for which the Egyptians were famous! Tiny treasures pulled from tombs and digs provide a glimpse into a rich and full society. Wall paintings and grave figurines wear ancient garments with eerily modern cuts—the body-conscious Egyptians were timeless in their style. This silk dress was inspired by a wood and plaster figure found in the tomb of Meket-re at Thebes. A matching silk scarf (page 114) drapes beautifully to create a pectoral-collar effect.

Skill Level
INTERMEDIATE

SIZE
To fit bust: 28 (32, 36, 40, 44)" (71 [81, 91, 101.5, 112] cm)

FINISHED MEASUREMENTS
Bust: 31½ (35½, 40, 44½, 53)" (80 [89, 101.5, 113, 134.5] cm)

Length: 66⅛ (67⅝, 69¼, 70¾, 73⅝)" (168 [172, 176, 180, 187] cm)

Note: See pattern tips for lengthening or shortening dress.

MATERIALS
Pure & Simple by Tilli Tomas (3½ oz [100 g] balls, each approx 260 yds [160 m], 100% silk)

A: Burnt Orange, 3 (3, 4, 4, 4) balls or 650 (715, 910, 962, 975) yds (593 [652, 830, 877, 889] m) worsted weight yarn

B: Crystal, 1 (1, 1, 1, 1) balls or 159 (169, 182, 196, 212) yds (145 [154, 166, 179, 193.5] m) worsted weight yarn

C: Moss, 1 (1, 1, 1, 1) balls or 91 (96, 104, 112, 121) yds (83 [87.5, 95, 102, 110.5] m) worsted weight yarn

D: Ruby Wine, 1 (1, 1, 1, 1) balls or 91 (96, 104, 112, 121) yds (83 [87.5, 95, 102, 110.5] m) worsted weight yarn

E: Glazed Ginger, 1 (1, 2, 2, 2) balls or 239 (253, 273, 294, 318) yds (218 [230.5, 249, 268, 290] m) worsted weight yarn

Size 4 (3.5 mm) circular needle at least 24" (61 cm) long, or size to obtain gauge

Stitch markers

Stitch holder

Safety pin

Darning needle

GAUGE
6 sts and 6 rows = 1" (2.5 cm) in chevron pattern

Refer to glossary on page 136 for: CCO, DKSS, I-Cord BO, K2togL, P2tog, VDD, WYIF, and YO.

RIBBED HEM
With A, cast on 188 (214, 240, 240, 266) sts.

Work 2 rows in garter st, then set up hem ribbing and back slit as follows:

NEXT ROW (RS): K1, wyif sl 1 (Chart A [DKSS Edge]), k1, place marker, work row 1 of Chart C (Rib Pattern) 14 (16, 18, 18, 20) times, place marker, k1, wyif sl 1, k1 [DKSS edge].

NEXT ROW (WS): Wyif sl 1, k1, wyif sl 1, sm, work back across ribbing as est to marker, sm, wyif sl 1, k1, wyif sl 1. Rep last 2 rows until ribbing measures 7¾ (7¾, 8¼, 8¾, 9¼)" (20 [20, 21, 22, 23] cm) from cast-on or desired length. For a shorter dress, this is a good place to adjust length. End with a WS row.

START CHEVRON PATTERN

NEXT ROW (RS): With A, k1, wyif sl 1, k1 [DKSS edge], sm. With B, work Row 1 of Chart B (Chevron Lace Pattern) 14 (16, 18, 18, 20) times to last 3 sts in row, join 2nd ball of A and k1, wyif sl 1, k1 [DKSS edge].

NEXT ROW (WS): With A, wyif sl 1, k1, wyif sl 1, with B work Row 2 of Chart B to last 3 sts, with A, wyif sl 1, k1, wyif sl 1.

Continue working edge sts in A. Work rem sts in Chart B changing colors as follows:

2 rows B

6 rows C

2 rows B

6 rows A

2 rows B

6 rows D

2 rows B

6 rows E

Side leg slit detail.

Work even in stripe pat and Chart B until piece measures 17½ (17½, 17¾, 17¾, 18)" (44.5 [44.5, 45, 45, 45.5] cm) from cast-on. This is another good place to adjust length.

NEXT ROW (RS): Slip 3 edge sts to safety pin to work later, cut both strands of A. Work as est in Chart B to last 3 sts, slip these last 3 sts to safety pin. Join work, placing marker to note start of round (side of dress)—182 (208, 234, 260, 312) sts rem on needle.

BEGIN WORKING IN THE ROUND

Cont working in Chart B as est, working in the round and switching to Rows 3 and 4 of pat to close the YO increases at desired point for personal modesty.

Work in Chart B until piece measures 28⅜ (28⅜, 28½, 28½, 28⅝)" (72.8 [72.8, 73.1, 73.1, 73.4] cm) from start of colorwork, or desired length. Piece should sit just above the hips.

End with 2 rounds of B in Chart B.

WAIST

NEXT ROUND: With A, work Row 1 of Chart C 14 (16, 18, 18, 20, 24) times around all sts.

Cont in rib pat as est until Waist ribbing measures 8¾ (8¾, 9, 9, 9¼)" (22 [22, 23, 23, 23.5] cm), end with Round 2 of chart. Once again, if you need to lengthen or shorten the dress, this is a good place to do so.

UNDERBUST

Return to Chart B (Rounds 3 and 4 of chart only), starting with 2 rounds of B and cont with colors as est in hip area until bust color area measures 5½ (5¾, 6, 6¼, 6½)" (14 [14.5, 15, 16, 16.5] cm), end with Round 4 of chart. End with Round 3 in B.

ARMHOLE SHAPING

From this point you will be working back and forth, working Chart A at Armhole edges as at edge of slit at bottom of dress.

NEXT ROW (WS): Cont with B, work Row 4 of Chart B as est across next 91 (104, 117, 130, 156) sts, place rem 91 (104, 117, 117, 130) sts on holder to work later.

NEXT ROW (RS): Cont in colors as in stripe pat, k1, wyif sl 1, k1 [DKSS Edge], p1, place marker, k2togL, k6, pm, work Row 1 of Chart B as est over next 65 (78, 91, 104, 130) sts 5 (6, 7, 8, 10) times, pm, k6, pm, p1, k1, wyif sl 1, k1 [DKSS Edge].

NEXT ROW (WS): Wyif sl 1, k1, wyif sl 1 [DKSS Edge], k1, sm, p2tog, p to marker, work Row 2 of Chart B as est to next marker, k1, wyif sl 1, k1, wyif sl 1 [DKSS Edge]. Rep last 2 rows, working only Rows 1 and 2 of Chart B. When fewer than 13 sts are left in any rep of Chart B, work those sts in St st. Cont in this manner until 55 (60, 73, 65, 74) sts total rem on needle. End with a WS row.

I-CORD BIND-OFF

NEXT ROW (RS): Cast on 2 sts at start of row using Cable Cast-On.

(K2, k2togL. Slip 3 sts from right-hand needle back onto left-hand needle. Pull yarn taut across back of work.) Repeat across work until 3 sts rem, k3togL, pull yarn tail through loop. Fasten off.

Slip sts from holder onto needle and work Front as for Back.

TIES

Try dress on and determine length of shoulder ties. Make 2 pieces of 3-st I-cord and stitch in place at corners of Front and Back.

CHART A
DKSS EDGE

CHART B
CHEVRON LACE PATTERN

4 Rows 3 & 4
3 Closed Chevron
2 Rows 1 & 2 Open
1 Lattice Chevron

13 12 11 10 9 8 7 6 5 4 3 2 1

CHART C
RIB PATTERN

13 12 11 10 9 8 7 6 5 4 3 2 1

| | Knit 1
Ⅴ Slip stitch with yarn in front
V Slip stitch
Ⴍ Twist 1 stitch
O Yarn over
△ Vertical double decrease

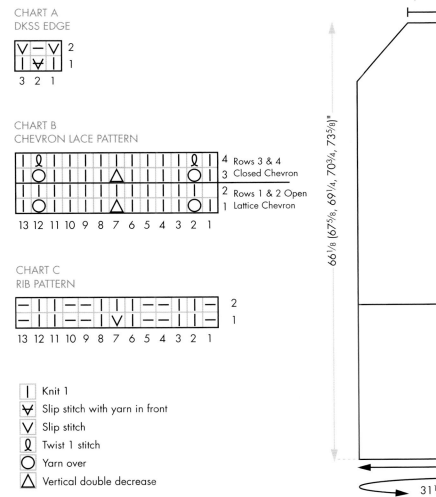

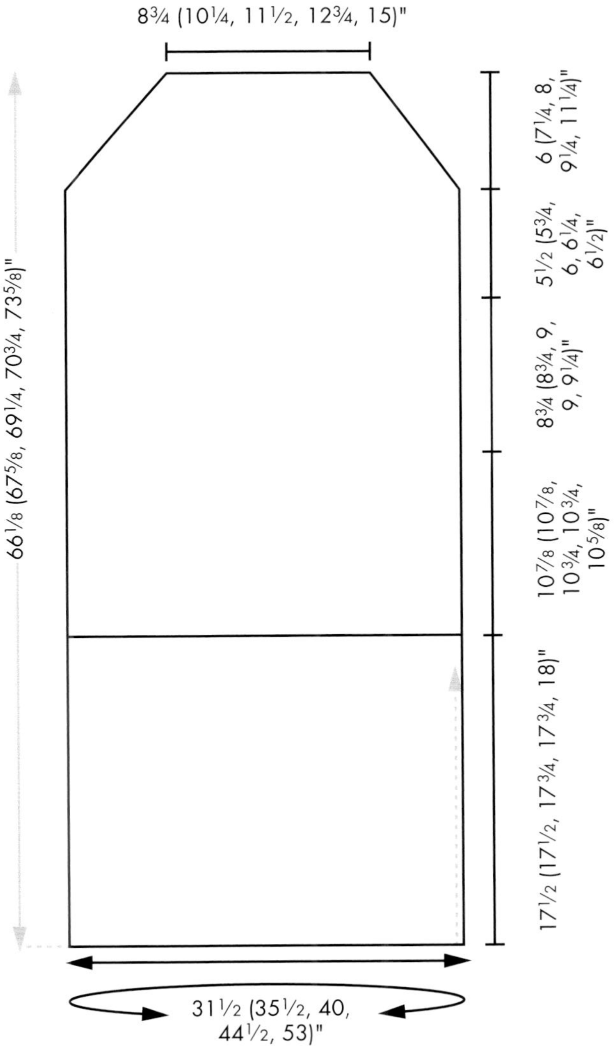

8¾ (10¼, 11½, 12¾, 15)"

6 (7¼, 8, 9¼, 11¼)"

5½ (5¾, 6, 6¼, 6½)"

8¾ (8¾, 9, 9, 9¼)"

10⅞ (10⅞, 10¾, 10¾, 10⅝)"

17½ (17½, 17¾, 17¾, 18)"

66⅛ (67⅝, 69¼, 70¾, 73⅝)"

31½ (35½, 40, 44½, 53)"

Jezebel

We all need to be a little naked sometimes—a flirty skirt, a little shoulder action, some cleavage—it's the froth on the latte at the cafe of romance. The yarn used in this halter slip dress has so much memory it should be in therapy; it stretches and hugs and does magnificent things when it's worked in ribbing. The top of the dress is worked first, then the stitches at the bottom of the ribbed waist section are picked up and the skirt is knit down to the hem. Like a longer skirt? Just keep knitting! Optional crocheted chain edging adds to the flirty, frothy appeal of this sexy dress.

Skill Level
INTERMEDIATE

SIZE
To fit bust: 30 (33, 36, 40, 44, 50)" (76 [84, 91, 101.5, 112, 127] cm)

FINISHED MEASUREMENTS
Waist: 23 (26, 29, 33, 37, 43)" (58.5 [66, 74, 84, 94, 119] cm)

Hem Circumference: 46 (52, 58, 66, 74, 86)" (117 [132, 147.5, 167.5, 188, 218.5] cm)

Length: 20¼ (22, 23¾, 25¾, 27, 28¼)" (51.5 [56, 60, 65.5, 68.5, 71.5] cm)

MATERIALS
Suede Deluxe by Berroco (1¾ oz [50 g] skeins, each approx 100 yds [92 m], 85% nylon, 10% rayon, 5% polyester), Tonto Gold 3920, 11 (11, 11, 12, 12, 13) skeins or 556 (589, 622, 663, 707, 753) yds (507 [537, 567, 605, 638.5, 687] m) worsted weight yarn

Size 7 (4.5 mm) circular needle at least 20" (51 cm) long, or size to obtain gauge

Size 8 (5 mm) double-pointed needles (dpn)

Additional circular needles in sizes 8 (5 mm), 9 (5.5 mm), 10 (6 mm), 10½ (6.5 mm), and 13 (9 mm)

See Circular Stress page 112 for thoughts on circular needle lengths.

Size K/10½ (6.5 mm) crochet hook

Darning needle

Stitch markers

GAUGE
6 sts and 7 rows = 1" (2.5 cm) over k2, p2 rib, relaxed as knitted

4.5 sts and 7 rows = 1" (2.5 cm) over k2, p2 rib, stretched as worn

Refer to glossary on page 136 for: DKSS, K2, P2 Rib, K2togL, K2togR, K2tog Picot Bind-Off, Sl st, W&T, YO, and YYK. See page 47 for crochet techniques: Ch, Sl st crochet.

This dress is designed for a size B bra cup, but directions are given in the pattern to increase the cup size to a C or D by additional short-row shaping.

WAIST RIBBING
Using a provisional cast-on, CO 102 (114, 130, 146, 166, 190) sts.
ROUND 1 (RS): (K2, p2); rep to end of row, end k2.
Cont in rib as est for 1" (2.5 cm).

TUMMY SHORT-ROW SHAPING

Work 53 (59, 67, 75, 85, 97) sts, W&T, work 4 sts in rib as est, W&T. Work to the 2 sts past the center st, then turn and work 4 sts back so the first two W&Ts are exactly 2 sts from either side of the center point of the waistband.

(Work to 4 sts past last wrapped st, slipping wrap up to needle and working with wrapped st, W&T); rep until 29 (31, 35, 39, 49, 57) sts rem each edge.

Cont in rib as est, working back and forth across all sts until side measures 1½ (2, 2½, 3, 3¼, 3½)" (3.8 [5, 6.5, 7.5, 8.5, 9] cm).

RIB CAGE SHORT ROWS

Work 53 (59, 67, 75, 85, 97) sts, W&T, work 2 sts in rib as est, W&T.

(Work to 4 sts past last wrapped st, slipping wrap up to needle and working with wrapped st, W&T); rep until 29 (27, 31, 31, 33, 37) sts rem each edge.

Work 2 rows in rib as est, working back and forth across all sts. End with a WS row, inc 2 sts in last row of ribbing—104 (116, 132, 148, 168, 192) sts.

I-CORD BIND-OFF AND TRIM

Work I-cord bind-off across next 24 (26, 30, 30, 36, 40) sts, work horizontal I-cord across next 56 (64, 72, 88, 96, 112) sts, work I-cord bind-off across last 24 (26, 30, 30, 36, 40) sts.

Cut yarn.

CUPS

Cont with rem live sts, divide sts in half for 2 cups, using a separate ball of yarn for each cup—28 (32, 36, 44, 48, 56) sts each cup. Cups will be worked in St st. Work both cups at the same time, step by step, with 2 balls of yarn, as follows:

RIGHT CUP

ROW 1 (RS): K1, wyif sl 1, k1, p2 [DKSS edge], (k2, m1) 5 times, knit to last 5 sts, k1, wyif sl 1, k1, p2.
ROWS 2 AND 4: Wyif sl 1, k1, wyif sl 1 [DKSS edge], p to last 5 sts, wyif sl 1, k1, wyif sl 1.

ROW 3: Work DKSS edges as est, (k3, m1) 5 times, knit to last 5 stitches, DKSS edge—38 (42, 46, 54, 58, 66) sts.

LEFT CUP

ROWS 1 AND 3 (RS): K1, wyif sl 1, k1, p2 [DKSS edge], knit to last 5 sts, K1, wyif sl 1, k1, p2.
ROW 2 (RS): Wyif sl 1, k1, wyif sl 1 [DKSS edge], (p2, m1) 5 times, purl to last 5 sts, work DKSS edge across last 5 sts.
ROW 4 (RS): Wyif sl 1, k1, wyif sl 1 [DKSS edge], (p3, m1) 5 times, purl to last 5 sts, work DKSS edge across last 5 sts—38 (42, 46, 54, 58, 66) sts.

RIGHT CUP SHORT-ROW SHAPING

SHORT ROW 1 (RS): Work 19 (21, 23, 27, 29, 33) sts across Right Cup as est, W&T.
SHORT ROWS 2 AND 4 (WS): Work back to start of row, working DKSS edge as est.
SHORT ROW 3 (RS): Work to 2 sts before last wrapped st, W&T.
Rep Short Rows 3 and 4 three more times.

LEFT CUP SHORT-ROW SHAPING

NEXT ROW (RS): Work DKSS edge as est, knit to last 5 sts (dealing with wraps as before), work DKSS edge as est.
SHORT ROW 1 (WS): Work 19 (21, 23, 27, 29, 33) sts across Left Cup as est, W&T.
SHORT ROWS 2 AND 4 (RS): Work back to start of row, working DKSS edge as est.
SHORT ROW 3 (WS): Work to 2 sts before last wrapped st, W&T.
Rep Short Rows 3 and 4 three more times.

CROSSING CENTER DKSS EDGES

NEXT ROW (RS): Work DKSS edge as est, knit to last 5 sts, slipping wraps onto needle and working along with wrapped st to avoid a hole at each short row, do not work DKSS edge yet.
Slip DKSS edge sts from Right Cup to dpn and hold to back, work first 5 sts of Left Cup as est onto separate dpn. Pass DKSS Right Cup sts between Left Cup sts just

worked and the rest of Left Cup, and work them as est with right-hand needle.

Slip Left Cup DKSS sts from dpn onto right-hand needle, then work knit to last 5 sts, dealing with wraps in same manner as for Right Cup, work DKSS edge as est.

NEXT ROW (WS): Work DKSS edge as est, work to last 5 sts of Left Cup, work DKSS as est, rep for Right Cup.

Work 4 rows with no shaping. For C cup repeat short-row shaping once, for D cup repeat short-row shaping twice.

RIGHT CUP DECREASE

ROW 1 (RS): Work 19 (21, 23, 27, 29, 33) sts, k2togR, pm, work to end of row.

ROWS 2 AND 4 (WS): Work in pat as est.

ROW 3: Work to 2 sts before marker, k2togR, work to end of row.

Rep Rows 3 and 4 until 29 (33, 37, 45, 49, 57) sts rem in cup.

LEFT CUP DECREASE

ROW 1 (RS): Work in pat as est to end of row.

ROW 2 (WS): Work 19 (21, 23, 27, 29, 33) sts, pm, p2togR, work to end of row as est.

ROW 3 (RS): Work in pat as est.

ROW 4 (WS): Work to marker, sm, p2togR, work to end of row as est.

Rep Rows 3 and 4 until 29 (33, 37, 45, 49, 57) sts rem in cup.

CENTERED BUST DECREASE

NEXT ROW (RS): Work DKSS edge, k1 (3, 5, 9, 11, 15) sts, place marker, work Row 1 of Halter Dress Chart across next 17 sts, pm, k3 (3, 7, 9, 11, 15) sts, work DKSS edge. Rep for Left Cup.

Work sts between markers in Row 2–12 of chart, while continuing to work outer sts as est.

Work 13th and 14th Chart Rows 3 (3, 7, 9, 11, 15) times until there is no st between marker and DKSS edge.

Work Chart Rows 15–20, then rep Rows 19 and 20 until straps are long enough to reach around neck and tie.

SKIRT

With size 7 needles, pick up each provisionally cast-on st—104 (116, 132, 148, 168, 192) sts.

ROUND 1 (RS): Starting at the center back and working in the round, knit.

NEXT ROUND: *K4 (4, 6, 7, 7, 8) sts, inc 1 into next st, knit same st; rep from * 28 (28, 24, 20, 24, 24) times around work, end k4 (16, 20, 20, 12, 12)—132 (144, 156, 168, 192, 216) sts total. Place marker to note start of round.

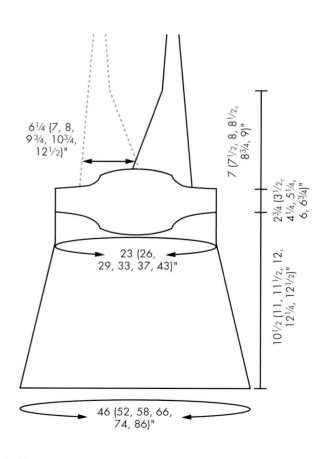

ESTABLISH SLIP STITCH PATTERN

NEXT ROUND: *K11 (12, 13, 14, 16, 18) sts , sl 1 st; rep from * 12 times around all sts.

NEXT ROUND: Knit.

Rep last 2 rounds 5 times.

Switch to size 8 needles and rep last 2 rounds 5 times.

Switch to size 9 needles and rep last 2 rounds 5 times.

Switch to size 10 needles and rep last 2 rounds 3 times.

NEXT ROUND: *K5 (5, 6, 6, 7, 8), YO, k5 (6, 6, 7, 8, 9) sl 1; rep from * 12 times around work—144 (156, 168, 180, 204, 228) sts total.

NEXT ROUND: K6 (7, 7, 8, 9, 10), *p1, k11 (12, 13, 14, 16, 18); rep from * 11 times around work, end K6 (6, 7, 7, 8, 9).

NEXT ROUND: *K5 (6, 6, 7, 7, 8), wyif sl 1, k6 (5, 6, 6, 8, 9), sl 1; rep from * 12 times around work.

Switch to size 10½ needles and rep last 2 rounds 5 times.

Switch to size 13 needles and rep last 2 rounds 5 times.

Switch to size 10½ needles, YYK all sts.

NEXT ROUND: Work each st as a YYK, knitting only one loop of each prev YYK.

Rep last round until skirt measures 5" (12.5 cm) above knee, or desired length. BO all sts very loosely with K2tog picot BO, chaining 5 sts between each BO st.

CROCHETED EDGING

(Sl st into next ch5 picot BO loop, ch5); rep, working in a spiral around all ch5-spaces, until picot ruffle is desired length.

FINISHING

Sew straps together so that cups fit snugly. If desired, tack bottom outer edges of cups to ribbing for a bit more support.

Weave in ends, steam-block.

	Knit 1
⅄	Slip stitch with yarn in front
V	Slip stitch
—	Purl 1
◣	Purl 2 together with a left slant
△	Vertical double decrease
◿	Knit 2 together with a right slant
◺	Knit 2 together with a left slant
O	Yarn over
◭	Quad double decrease

CHART A
HALTER DRESS
Green shaded sts represent DKSS edge.
Gray sts are deleted sts.

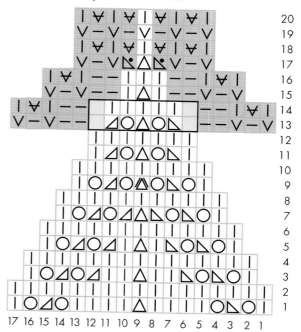

Accessories

"God is in the details." —Mies van der Rohe

Fashion detailing is vital to complete a romantic look. There is no substitute for the power of a well-chosen shawl or a pair of gloves to bring an entire outfit together.

Women used to spend more money on hats than on any other part of their wardrobes. Fashionable, well-chosen millinery can make any woman look like a queen (which may be why Queen Elizabeth owns so many hats). In France, women have the innate ability to drape a piece of fabric around their necks, adding allure and inviting romance with each turn of the head.

Handknit accessories are a treasure to give and receive, and they are a joy to work up. The ability to express ourselves so easily, so delicately, is a gift that nonknitters look on with envy. Here is a collection of several of my favorite fashion furnishings, which will add a sense of romance to any wardrobe.

Silk Stockings

The thing about silk is that it's—silky! It has a drape and a sheen unlike any other fiber, but it lacks memory. Perhaps it's all that time spent as a cocoon; it's locked everything away and doesn't want to look back. To give these silk long stockings a bit more elasticity, they're worked in a rib and lace pattern that starts above the toe and wanders up to the thigh. You can wear them with a garter belt or sew elastic into the tops, creating a self-supporting thigh-high stocking.

Skill Level
INTERMEDIATE

SIZE
Women's S (M, L)

FINISHED MEASUREMENTS
Foot Circumference: 7 (7¾, 8½)" 18 [19, 21.5] cm)

Foot Length: 7½ (8½, 9½)" (19 [20, 24] cm)

Leg Length: 19⅛ (21¾, 24⅜)" (49 [54.5, 62] cm)

MATERIALS
Regal Silk 101 by Artyarns (1¾ oz [50 g] skeins, each approx 163 yds [149m], 100% silk), White/Pink 221, 2 (2, 2) balls or 289 (326, 381) yds (263.5 [297.5, 347.5] m) sportweight yarn

Size 5 (3.75 mm), 2 circular needles 12" (30.5 cm) long, or size to obtain gauge.

See Circular Stress page 112 for thoughts on circular needle lengths.

Darning needle

Stitch markers

GAUGE
6 sts and 7 rows = 1" (2.5 cm) over St st using smaller needles

Refer to glossary on page 136 for: Circ, K2togL, K2togR, Sl st, VDD, W&T, and YO.

This pattern is written to be worked on 2 circular needles. For ease of comprehension, one needle is designated as the "Sole" and the other as the "Instep" needle.

TOE

Holding 2 smaller circular needles parallel in your right hand, cast on 12 (12, 12) sts by casting on 1 stitch on one needle, then casting on 1 st on the other needle 6 times. Work back and forth, holding the circs close together, until all sts are cast on.

ROUND 1: Always working the sts on circ #1 with the opposite end of circ #1, k1, knit into the back, then into the front of the next st, knit to the last 2 sts on circ #1, knit into the back and front of the next st, knit the last st. Move to circ #2 and repeat.

ROUND 2: Always working the sts with the opposite end of the same needle on which they sit, knit all sts.

Repeat the last 2 rounds until there are 44 (48, 52) sts total, then repeat only Round 2, working even with no shaping until sock reaches just past small toe—22 (24, 26) sts on each needle.

Designate one needle as the Instep, and dec 1 st in center of Instep needle in final "toe round"—21 (23, 25) sts.

Slip 2 (1, 0) sts from each edge of Sole needle onto Instep needle—18 (22, 26) Sole sts and 25 Instep sts.

The garter edge can be held up with a garter belt or turned under and hemmed to create a casing for wide elastic.

LACE INSTEP

Beg with st 1, Row 1 of Chart A (Instep Lace Top/Front Panel), work 25 Instep needle sts in pat while working rem 18 (22, 26) sts on Sole needle in St st.

Cont in pats as est until piece measures 5¼ (6, 6¾)" (13.5 [15.4, 17.3] cm), or until piece reaches center point of ankle bone.

SHORT-ROW HEEL PART I (WORKED ONLY ON SOLE NEEDLE, ST ST SECTION)

ROW 1 (RS): On Sole needle only, knit to last st, W&T.

ROW 2 (WS): On Sole needle only, purl to last st, W&T.

ROW 3: Cont in St st as est, work to 1 st before last wrapped st, W&T.

Rep Row 3 until 6 sts rem unwrapped in center of Sole needle, end with a RS Row.

NEXT ROW (WS): Knit to end of Sole needle, slipping the wrap from each st up onto left-hand needle and working it, along with the st it was wrapped around, together as a purl st. Turn work.

NEXT ROUND (RS): Knit to end of Sole needle, working wraps as in previous row, knitting all sts on needle. Continue around sts on Instep needle in lace pat as est.

SHORT-ROW HEEL PART II (WORKED ONLY ON SOLE NEEDLE)

ROW 1 (RS): Work 14 (15, 16) sts, W&T.

ROW 2 (WS): P3 sts, W&T.

ROW 3: Cont in St st, work to 1 st past last wrapped st, working wrap along with stitch as previously done, W&T. Rep Row 3 until all sts have been worked, end with a WS row.

ANKLE

NEXT ROUND: Work around all sts, working sts on Instep needle in lace pat as est, and working sts on Sole needle as follows:

Work 3 sts in Row 1 of Chart C (Side Edges), pm, work 12 (16, 20) in Chart B (Sole/Back of Leg Ribbing), starting and ending where directed for your size, pm, work last 3 sts on Sole needle Chart C.

Cont in pats as est until sock reaches just beyond narrow portion of ankle—3⅜ (3¾, 4⅛)" (8.5 [9.5, 10.5] cm) from end of heel shaping.

NEXT ROUND: Work to marker, sm, YO, work to marker, YO, sm, work rem sts in pats as est.

NEXT 3 ROUNDS: Work in pats as est, working inc sts into leg back ribbing.

Cont inc in this manner, inc 2 sts every 4 rounds, until there are 120 (132, 144) sts total.

LEG

Work even until stocking reaches midthigh—19⅛ (21¾, 24⅜)" (48.5 [55, 62] cm) from end of heel shaping.

GARTER TOP

Work 6 rounds in garter st (knit 1 round, purl 1 round) twice.

BIND OFF

PREPARATION ROUND: (K1, sl 1); rep around all sts.

BO ROUND: BO all sts *loosely* using a larger needle.

CHART A
INSTEP
LACE TOP/FRONT PANEL

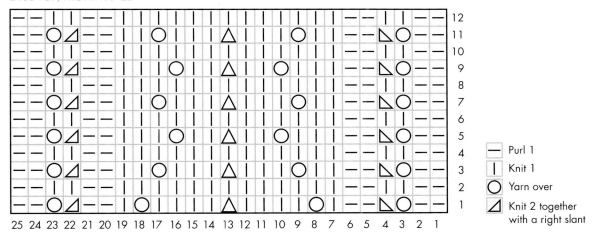

— Purl 1

| Knit 1

O Yarn over

◿ Knit 2 together with a right slant

CHART C
SIDE EDGES

CHART B
SOLE/BACK OF LEG RIBBING

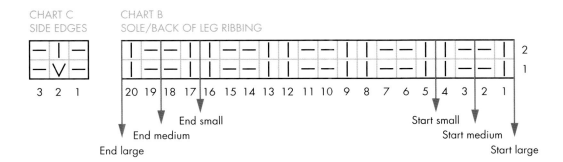

Some Like It Hot

Favored by high society dames and strippers alike, the ubiquitous long opera glove was a mainstay of the 1950s martini and cigarette nightclub scene. Marilyn wore them, so did Audrey, Sophia, Grace, and Kim. But the most memorable were those worn by Rita Hayworth while singing "Zip!" in the 1957 film *Pal Joey*. A lace panel runs the length of these black gloves worked in a blend of cotton and lycra. Optional elastic at the upper arm holds them in place.

Skill Level
EASY

SIZE
Women's S (M, L)

FINISHED MEASUREMENTS
Bicep: 12½ (13½, 14¾)" (32 [34.5,37.5] cm)

Wrist: 6½ (7½, 8¾)" (16.5 [19, 22] cm)

Cuff Length: 11 (13,15)" (28 [33, 38] cm)

MATERIALS
Fixation by Cascade (1¾ oz [50 g] balls, each approx 100 yds (92 m), 98.3% cotton, 1.7% elastic), Black 8990, 3 (3, 3) balls or 266 (303, 337) yds (242.5 [273.5, 307.5] m) sportweight yarn

Size 3 (3.25 mm) double-pointed needles

Size 4 (3.5 mm) double-pointed needles, or size to obtain gauge

Stitch holders

Stitch markers

Darning needle

¼" (6 mm) elastic

Sewing thread for tacking ends of elastic cuffs

GAUGE
5 sts and 6.5 rows = 1" (2.5 cm) over St st using larger needles

Refer to glossary on page 136 for: K2togL, K2togR, M1, P2togL, P2togR, St st, PU&K, VDD, and YO.

CUFF

With smaller needles, CO 63 (69, 75) sts, dividing sts evenly—21 (23, 25) sts on each needle. Join to work in the round.

With smaller needles knit 6 rounds. Change to larger needles, purl 1 round.

Starting with Row 17 (9,1) of charts, work Chart A (Glove Lace Back) on needle 1, then work Row 17 (9,1) of Chart B (Glove Front) across needle 2 and needle 3.

Cont in pats as est, working dec as directed until 11 (13,15) sts rem on each needle—33 (39, 45) sts.

Work even with no further decreasing, cont in Chart A pat on needle 1 and work in ribbing as est on needles 2 and 3 until piece measures 11 (13, 15)" (28 [33, 38] cm) from cast-on or desired length to wrist.

NEXT ROUND: Cont in pat as est on needle 1; on needles 2 and 3 work to center st (VDD st from prev round), m1, work to end of needle—35 (41,47) sts.

Cont working needle 1 in lace pat with no decs (Chart C [Lace]), and begin working needles 2 and 3 in St st for 4 rounds.

NEXT ROUND: Cont in pat as est on needle 1; on needles 2 and 3 work to center st (VDD st from prev

round), m1, work to end of needle—37 (43, 49) sts. Rep last 4 rounds once more—39 (45, 51) sts.

THUMB OPENING

RIGHT THUMB: Cont as est on needle 1, work 4 (4, 5) sts on needle 2, with a piece of waste yarn k7 (8, 9) sts, slip these back to needle and knit to end of needle 2. Knit to last 4 (4, 5) sts on needle 3, place marker, work to end of round.

LEFT THUMB: Cont as est on needle 1, work 4 (4, 5) sts on needle 2, place marker and knit to end of needle 2. Knit to last 11 (12, 14) sts on needle 3, with a piece of waste yarn k7 (8, 9) sts, slip these back to needle, work to end of round.

You now have 19 (22, 25) sts for the palm and 20 (23, 26) sts for the back of the hand. Cont working lace as est and all other sts in St st until hand measures 1½ (2, 2½)" (3.8 [5, 6.5] cm) from start of Thumb, or until hand portion reaches base of fingers.

PALM TOP

Divide sts in half at marker and outside of Thumb—19 (22, 25) Palm sts, 20 (23, 26) hand back sts. Place sts from each section on a separate piece of waste yarn.

THUMB

Insert dpn into 7 (8, 9) sts above and below Thumb marking waste yarn, remove yarn. Pick up 1 additional st on either side of Thumb—16 (18, 20) sts.

Divide sts between 3 dpns and work in St st for approx 1¼" (3 cm) until Thumb reaches knuckle.

Dec 1 st at palm side of Thumb, cont until Thumb is desired length, k1 (k2tog); rep around all sts.

Break yarn, leaving an 8" (20 cm) tail and draw through all sts.

INDEX FINGER

Slip 5 (6, 7) sts from palm waste yarn and 6 (7, 8) sts from hand back waste yarn onto dpns. Knit to space between fingers, CO 2 sts, knit to end of round—13 (15,17) sts.

Knit around until Finger reaches first knuckle, dec 1 st at palm side of Finger. Cont until Finger reaches second

knuckle, dec 1 st at back side of Finger.

Cont until Finger reaches just below tip of finger, k1, (k2togR); rep to end of round.

Break yarn, leaving an 8" (20 cm) tail and draw through rem sts.

MIDDLE FINGER

Slip 5 (6, 7) sts from each waste yarn onto dpns. Knit across back of Finger, CO 3 sts, knit across front of Finger, PU&K 2 sts from prev CO sts, knit to end of round—15 (17, 19) sts.

Knit around until Finger reaches first knuckle, dec 1 st at palm side of Finger. Cont until Finger reaches second knuckle, dec 1 st at back side of Finger.

Cont until Finger reaches just below tip of finger, k1, (k2togR); rep to end of round.

Break yarn, leaving an 8" (20 cm) tail and draw through all sts.

RING FINGER

Slip 5 (5, 6) sts from each waste yarn onto dpns. Knit across back of Finger, CO 3 sts, knit across front of Finger, PU&K 3 sts from prev CO sts, knit to end of round—16 (16, 18) sts.

Knit around until Finger reaches first knuckle, dec 1 st at palm side of Finger. Cont until Finger reaches second knuckle, dec 1 st at back side of Finger.

Cont until Finger reaches just below tip of finger, k1, (k2togR); rep to end of round.

Break yarn, leaving an 8" (20 cm) tail and draw through all sts.

PINKIE FINGER

Slip 4 (5, 5) sts from each waste yarn onto dpns. Knit across back of Finger, knit across front of Finger, pick up 3 sts from prev CO sts, knit to end of round—11 (13, 13) sts.

Knit around until Finger reaches first knuckle, dec 1 st at palm side of Finger. Cont until Finger reaches second knuckle, dec 1 st at back side of Finger.

Cont until Finger reaches just below tip of finger, k1, (k2togR), rep to end of round.

Break yarn, leaving an 8" (20 cm) tail and draw through all sts.

FINISHING

Turn cast-on edge under and sew in place to create facing, leaving a ½" (13 mm) space. Insert a ¼" (6 mm) elastic, cut to the circumference of bicep plus 1" (2.5 cm), sew together.

With a darning needle, draw ends into fingers and weave in place.

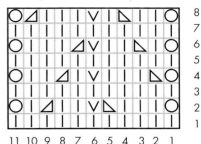

CHART C
LACE (NO DECREASING)

O	Yarn over
⟋	Knit 2 together with a right slant
I	Knit 1
V	Slip stitch
⟍	Knit 2 together with a left slant
⟍•	Purl 2 together with a right slant
⟍•	Purl 2 together with a left slant
△	Vertical double decrease

CHART A
GLOVE LACE BACK (1 PANEL)

CHART B
GLOVE FRONT (2 PANELS)

Stop Dec Size S
11 sts each needle
Work even from this point no further dec

Stop Dec Size M
13 sts each needle
Work even from this point no further dec

Stop Dec Size L
15 sts each needle
Work even from this point no further dec

Start Size S

Start Size M

Start Size L

June Bride

Silk Mohair worked in an elegant lace pattern makes these deceptively simple short lace mitts a joy to work up. Wear them on chilly days when your hands are cold but you need to use your fingers (for knitting, perhaps?) or wear them to show off your lace skills!

Skill Level
INTERMEDIATE

SIZE
Women's S (M, L)

FINISHED MEASUREMENTS
Wrist: 6½ (7½, 8¾)" (16.5 [19, 22] cm)

Palm: 5¼ (6½, 7¾)" (13 [16.5, 20] cm)

MATERIALS
Cashmere 5 by Artyarns (1¾ oz [50 g] skeins, each approx 102 yds [93 m] 100% Cashmere, 30% Silk), CS 128, 1 skein (all sizes)

Note: Use only 2 strands to create the mitts.

Size 5 (3.75 mm) double-pointed needles, or size needed to obtain gauge

Size F/5 (3.75 mm) crochet hook

Stitch markers

Darning needle

Safety pin

GAUGE
6 sts and 7.5 rows = 1" (2.5 cm) over St st

Refer to glossary on page 136 for: Garter st, K2togL, K2togR, K2tog Picot Bind-Off.

MITT CUFF

CO 80 (96, 112) sts.

Work 4 rows in garter st. Join, place marker to note start of round—this will be the center of the palm.

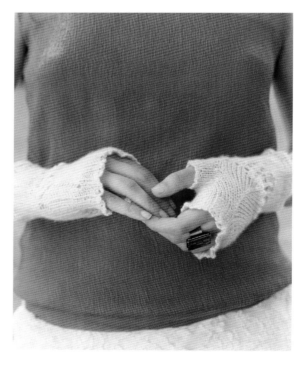

NEXT ROW: (K2togR); rep across work—40 (48, 56) sts.

NEXT 10 ROUNDS: Knit.

NEXT ROUND: K1, (p2, k2) 2 (3, 4) times, p2, k2togR, k16, p2, (k2, p2) 2 (3,4) times, k1—31 (39, 47) sts

Cont in pats as est for 3 more rounds.

ESTABLISH LACE PATTERN

NEXT ROUND: Work in ribbing as est across first 11 (15,19) sts, work Lace Mitts Chart across next 17 sts, work in rib pat as est to end of round. Cont in pats as est until rib section measures 1¼ (1½, 1¾)" (3.2 [3.8, 4.5] cm).

NEXT ROUND: Knit to start of chart, work in chart pat as est, knit to end of round.

Cont working chart as est, working all other sts in St st until piece measures 1¼ (1½, 1¾)" (3 [3.8, 4.5] cm) from end of rib section.

LEFT THUMB OPENING

NEXT ROUND: K3 (5,6) sts, with a piece of waste yarn k5 (6, 7) sts, slip these waste yarn sts back to left-hand needle and knit them again, work to chart and complete round as est.

Cont working as est, working center sts in charted pat and all other sts in St st, until piece measures 1½ (1¾, 2)" (3.8 [4.5, 5] cm) from start of work or reaches to base of fingers.

RIGHT THUMB OPENING

NEXT ROUND: Work 32 (37, 43) sts in pat as est, with a piece of waste yarn k5 (6, 7) sts, slip these waste yarn sts back to left-hand needle and knit them again, knit to end of round.

Cont working as est, working center sts in charted pat and all other sts in St st, until piece measures 1½ (1¾, 2)" (3.8 [4.5, 5] cm) from start of work or reaches to base of fingers.

TOP OF HAND

NEXT 2 ROUNDS: Knit all sts.
NEXT 4 ROUNDS: Work in garter st.
Work k2tog picot bind-off, chaining 3 sts between each BO st.

THUMB

Slip 6 (7, 8) sts from top of Thumb opening waste yarn and 5 (6, 7) sts from bottom of Thumb opening waste yarn onto dpns—11 (13,15) sts total.
Knit 8 rounds (or until Thumb reaches knuckle).

NEXT 2 ROUNDS: Knit all sts.
NEXT 4 ROUNDS: Work in garter st.
BO as for Hand.

FINISHING

Steam-block piece. Weave in ends. If desired, single crochet around cast-on and bound-off edges to add extra dimension to the ruffled edges.

LACE MITTS CHART

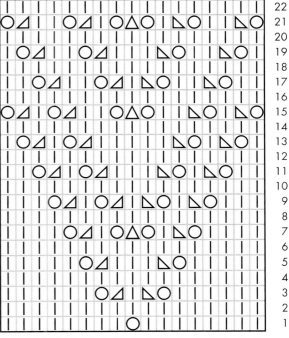

| | Knit 1
| O | Yarn over
| ∖ | Knit 2 together with a left slant
| △ | Vertical double decrease
| ╱ | Knit 2 together with a right slant

Gigi

One of the unsung joys of working lace is the bias movement of the stitches. Depending on the placement of the increases and decreases in this scarf, the panels appear to wave back and forth and from side to side. Edged with a Double Knit Slip Stitch technique that matches the I-cord cast-on and bind-off, this self-finishing wavy lace scarf can be worked to any length. It's a wonderful first lace project—after the first few rows you'll memorize the pattern and find it much easier than you might think!

Skill Level
INTERMEDIATE

SIZE
One size

FINISHED MEASUREMENTS
Width: 13" (33 cm)

Length: 52" (132 cm)

Dimensions are approximate. Exact size will vary based on knitting style and gauge variations.

MATERIALS
Disco Lights by Tilli Tomas (3½ oz (100 g) skeins, each approx 225 yds [205 m], 100% silk with sequins), Lime Cream, 2 balls or 450 yds (410 m) worsted weight yarn

Size 7 (4.5 mm) needles

Stitch markers

GAUGE
Approx 4 sts and 5 rows = 1" (2.5 cm) over Wavy Lace Pattern

Exact gauge is not important for this project.

Refer to glossary on page 136 for: DKSS, I-Cord BO, I-Cord Cast-On, K2togL, K2togR, Sl st, WYIF, and YO.

WAVY LACE PATTERN
See Chart A if you prefer to work from charts.

Multiple of 13 sts + 6

ROW 1: (K1, wyif sl 1, k1), (k3, YO, k1, p1, k4, k2togR, k2); rep to last 3 sts, (k1, wyif sl 1, k1).

ROW 2: (Wyif sl 1, k1, wyif sl 1), (p7, k1, p5); rep to last 3 sts, (wyif sl 1, k1, wyif sl 1).

ROW 3: (K1, wyif sl 1, k1), (k3, YO, k2, p1, k3, k2togR, k2); rep to last 3 sts, (k1, wyif sl 1, k1).

ROW 4: (Wyif sl 1, k1, wyif sl 1), (p6, k1, p6); rep to last 3 sts, (wyif sl 1, k1, wyif sl 1).

ROW 5: (K1, wyif sl 1, k1), (k3, YO, k3, p1, k2, k2togR, k2); rep to last 3 sts, (k1, wyif sl 1, k1).

ROW 6: (Wyif sl 1, k1, wyif sl 1), (p5, k1, p7); rep to last 3 sts, (wyif sl 1, k1, wyif sl 1).

ROW 7: (K1, wyif sl 1, k1), (k3, YO, k4, p1, k1, k2togR, k2); rep to last 3 sts, (k1, wyif sl 1, k1).

ROW 8: (Wyif sl 1, k1, wyif sl 1), (p4, k1, p8); rep to last 3 sts, (wyif sl 1, k1, wyif sl 1).

ROW 9: (K1, wyif sl 1, k1), (k3, YO, k5, p1, k2togR, k2); rep to last 3 sts, (k1, wyif sl 1, k1).

ROW 10: (Wyif sl 1, k1, wyif sl 1), (p3, k1, p9); rep to last 3 sts, (wyif sl 1, k1, wyif sl 1).

ROW 11: (K1, wyif sl 1, k1), (k3, k2togL, k4, p1, k1, YO, k2); rep to last 3 sts, (k1, wyif sl 1, k1).

ROW 12: (Wyif sl 1, k1, wyif sl 1), (p4, k1, p8); rep to last 3 sts, (wyif sl 1, k1, wyif sl 1).

ROW 13: (K1, wyif sl 1, k1), (k3, k2togL, k3, p1, k2, YO, k2); rep to last 3 sts, (k1, wyif sl 1, k1).

ROW 14: (Wyif sl 1, k1, wyif sl 1), (p5, k1, p7); rep to last 3 sts, (wyif sl 1, k1, wyif sl 1).

ROW 15: (K1, wyif sl 1, k1), (k3, k2togL, k2, p1, k3, YO, k2); rep to last 3 sts, (k1, wyif sl 1, k1).

ROW 16: (Wyif sl 1, k1, wyif sl 1), (p6, k1, p6); rep to last 3 sts, (wyif sl 1, k1, wyif sl 1).

ROW 17: (K1, wyif sl 1, k1), (k3, k2togL, k1, p1, k4, YO, k2); rep to last 3 sts, (k1, wyif sl 1, k1).

ROW 18: (Wyif sl 1, k1, wyif sl 1), (p7, k1, p5); rep to last 3 sts, (wyif sl 1, k1, wyif sl 1).

ROW 19: (K1, wyif sl 1, k1), (k3, k2togL, p1, k5, YO, k2); rep to last 3 sts, (k1, wyif sl 1, k1).

ROW 20: (Wyif sl 1, k1, wyif sl 1), (p8, k1, p4); rep to last 3 sts, (wyif sl 1, k1, wyif sl 1).

Rep Rows 1–20 for pat.

INSTRUCTIONS

Using I-cord cast-on, CO 58 sts.

NEXT ROW (WS): Wyif sl 1, k1, wyif sl 1, pm, p52 sts, pm, wyif sl 1, k1, wyif sl 1.

NEXT ROW (RS): Begin working Row 1 of Wavy Lace Pattern from chart or written instructions, work sts 1–3 for DKSS edge, sm, (work sts 4–16, pm); rep to last 3 sts, sm and work sts 17–19 to end row with DKSS edge. (Shown in yellow on chart.)

NEXT ROW (WS): Work pats as est, following chart or written instructions.

Cont working pat as est following charted or written instructions until all yarn is nearly used up, retaining approx 4 yds (3.7 m) for each st to complete the I-cord bind-off below.

FINISHING

Work I-cord bind-off across all sts.

Weave in ends.

Block to desired dimensions.

See Blocking with Steam, page 112, for more information on blocking.

LACE PATTERN CHART
Yellow sts denote DKSS edge.

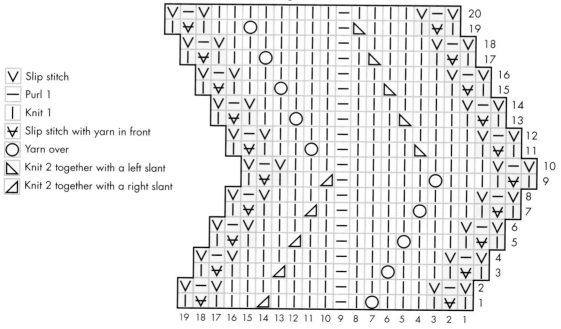

Key:
- V Slip stitch
- — Purl 1
- | Knit 1
- ⩔ Slip stitch with yarn in front
- O Yarn over
- ◺ Knit 2 together with a left slant
- ◿ Knit 2 together with a right slant

Basic Lace Knitting Techniques

Rather than be intimidated by lace, if we break it down into its simplest components we can learn to appreciate it and even design our own lace motifs. At its most basic level, lace is a series of paired increases and decreases within our knit fabric.

Unless the fabric is meant to become larger or smaller, each increase in a lace motif will have a paired decrease. The decreases are a series of stitches that are worked together and can slant in one of three ways: to the right, to the left, or straight up and down (no slant).

I much prefer charts to written lace patterns for a variety of reasons, the foremost being that a mistake is often easier to see in a chart than in written instructions. But I also understand that our minds work in different ways, and what may seem intuitive to me may not be so easy for someone else (and vice versa). For that reason I've included written instructions with many of the charts; I do hope that the more chart-fearful among you will at least compare your knitted lace to the chart and perhaps gain a more visual understanding of the beautiful movement of lace through the charts in this book!

BASIC LACE STITCH COMPONENTS

The basic increases and decreases of lace knitting are k2togR (knit 2 together with a right slant), k2togL (knit 2

together with a left slant), VDD (vertical double decrease), and YO (yarn over). For more information, consult the Stitch Glossary and Chart Symbol Key on page 136, and check out the many excellent lace knitting books available at most yarn and book shops. (See Recommended Reading on page 134 for a list of my favorites.)

BIAS

In woven fabric, *bias* is the directional fall of a fabric that has been cut at a 45-degree angle from the straight or *grain* of the fabric. Bias fabric is generally rather clingy and has more "give" than fabric cut on the grain.

In knitting, a *bias effect* is caused by introducing a distance of several stitches between an increase and its matching decrease.

Bias is an important component of lace knitting. Much of the beauty of a lace piece comes from the play of light moving from one lace section to another as the reflection from the different bias panels separates it visually from the other panels.

Creating interesting bias shapes in lacework is a way to create a "resting area" for the eye. It's easy for lacework to become too busy; it's sometimes nice to emphasize a delicate lace panel with several matching bias panels.

PLACEMENT OF BIAS SHAPING

It's interesting to note how the placement of the increases (YOs) and decreases, although vertical in a lace chart, may create a wavy bias effect due to the apparent movement of the stitches between the increases and decreases.

Stitches will appear to slant *from* the source of the increase *toward* the point of decrease, creating a wavy edge when used in alternate groups of rows. A wavy edge can be very nice in a scarf, on the edge of a pillowcase, or along the collar of a blouse.

Decreases must be balanced on either side of a multistitch increase to create a straight edge. Increases may also be balanced on either side of a multistitch decrease to achieve the same straight edge.

CIRCULAR STRESS

For many of these projects, circular needles are specified, with suggested lengths given. To be totally honest, I don't worry much about the lengths of the cables joining the tips of my circular needles—I tend to use the needle with the longest, most flexible cable I can find (Inox Express or Knitpicks Options needles are wonderful for this) and pull out an extra loop of cable to keep my stitches from becoming too stretched on the needle. Similar to the "Magic Loop" method, which has become popular over the past few years, I find it's a wonderful way to work a smaller tube with a longer needle. For this reason, I tend to place less emphasis on circular lengths when writing my patterns, which may seem unusual to some knitters.

The traditional rule of thumb for knitting in the round is to use a needle with a cable length that is smaller than the circumference of the knit garment. If this feels more comfortable to you as a knitter, then this is the way you should work—knitting should be fun and comfortable above all things!

I love double-pointed needles for very small areas, especially hat tips, glove fingers, and sock toes. I prefer wooden double points, but I love my long metal needles when working straight—we all have different needle preferences!

BLOCKING WITH STEAM

I prefer to block using steam whenever possible. For a larger garment, like the Holiday shawl on page 116, I lay a clean quilt on my dining room table and lay the shawl on top of that. I use a handheld Scunci® steamer for all of my blocking, but a good steam iron will do fine as long as you are careful not to touch the iron face to the fabric. Steam an area of the shawl, then, while it is hot and damp, gently tug it widthwise, then lengthwise, several times. This will help to even out the stitches. Allow the area just blocked to lie flat until completely cool (fewer than 5 minutes), then work on an adjoining section. Continue in this way until all sections of the garment are blocked. At this point I like to do a final full block of the garment, steaming the entire thing and allowing it to lie flat until totally cool.

Vertigo

This long scarf has a drape that intuitively wraps coil-like around the neck. Intended to complement Cleopatra on page 86, the scarf is worked in more luxurious yarns that boast a variety of sequins, semiprecious beads, and rhinestones that dress up a simple color-work pattern.

Skill Level
BEGINNER

SIZE
One size

FINISHED MEASUREMENTS
Width: 12" (30.5 cm)

Length: 67" (170 cm)

MATERIALS
A: Exotica by Tilli Tomas (3½ oz [100 g] skeins, each approx 225 yds [205 m], 100% silk with stone chips), Tiger Eye Rattan, 1 ball or 225 yds (205 m) worsted weight yarn

B: Mariel's Crystals by Tilli Tomas (1¾ oz [50 g] skeins, each approx 120 yds [110 m], 100% silk with Swarovski® crystals) Ruby Wine, 1 ball or 120 yds [110 m] worsted weight yarn

C: Disco Lights by Tilli Tomas (3½ oz [100 g] skeins, each approx 225 yds [205 m], 100% silk with sequins), Moss, 1 ball or 225 yds [205 m] worsted weight yarn

D: Ritz by Tilli Tomas (3½ oz [50 g] skeins, each approx 225 yds [205 m], 100% spun silk with beads and metallic thread), Ethereal, 1 ball or 125 yds [114 m] worsted weight yarn

E: Disco Lights by Tilli Tomas Burnt Orange, 1 ball or 225 yds [205 m] worsted weight yarn

F: Rock Star by Tilli Tomas (3½ oz [100 g] skeins, each approx 225 yds [205 m], 100% silk with beads) Ant, 2 balls or 550 yds (503m) worsted weight yarn

G: Pure & Simple by Tilli Tomas (1¾ oz [50 g] skeins, each approx 260 yds [137 m], 100% silk) or 260 yds (160 m) worsted weight yarn

Size 8 (5 mm), 36" (91 cm) long circular needle, or size to obtain gauge

Size G (4mm) crochet hook

GAUGE
4.75 sts and 6 rows = 1" (2.5 cm) over garter st with G

SCARF
Note: When starting a new strand or cutting yarns, leave a 10" (25.4 cm) tail to be knotted together with fringe during finishing. Cut yarns as directed at end of each color block section. Yarn B will not be cut throughout the scarf; strand B up along the edge of the work.

ROW 1: With one strand of A and one strand of B held together and using the long-tail cast-on (holding B to the front so it creates the bottom edge), cast on 320 sts.

ROWS 2 AND 3: Drop B, and with A, knit 2 rows. Cut A.

ROWS 4 AND 5: With B, knit 2 rows.

ROW 6: With C, purl 1 row.

ROW 7: With C, knit 1 row.

Rep Rows 6 and 7 twice more (6 rows of C total). Cut C.

ROW 12: With B, knit 1 row.

ROW 13: With D, purl 1 row.

ROW 14: With D, knit 1 row.

Rep Rows 13 and 14 once more (4 rows of D total). Cut D.

ROW 17: With B, knit 1 row.

ROWS 18–23: With E, rep Rows 6–11. Cut E.

ROW 24: Rep Row 12.

ROWS 25–28: With F, rep Rows 13–16. Cut F.

ROWS 29–31: With B, knit 3 rows.

ROWS 32–34: With A, knit 3 rows. Cut A.

ROWS 35–37: With B, knit 3 rows.

Rep Rows 6–28 once more.

With B, knit 2 rows.

With A, knit 2 rows.

Bind off loosely with B.

FINISHING

Weave in ends.

FRINGE (NOT SHOWN)

Cut G into 20" (52.5 cm) lengths and apply as fringe to either edge of scarf, attaching 1 folded strand (10" [25.4 cm] when folded) as directed to the edge of each row—60 strands of fringe on either edge of work.

To apply fringe, use a crochet hook and fold each fringe piece or group of fringes in half. Pull the center of a single piece of fringe through the cast-on or bound-off stitch, then pull the ends of the fringe through the loop, securing the fringe to the edge of the shawl.

Steam-block, combing fringe so it is straight, and cut along the bottom edges to even the fringe.

See Blocking with Steam, page 112, for more information on blocking.

# Holiday

I happened upon this amazing yarn at a tiny shop in Buffalo, New York, and it was love at first sight. I couldn't even wait for the store owner to help me before I'd slipped the yarn over the swift and wound a giant 400-yard ball of heaven. A yarn like this demands to be shown off, preferably in a very simple design with lots of room to glow. The lace triangle shawl is worked from a charted pattern. The increases are included in the chart and once one repeat is worked, the pattern is very easy to memorize. If you can't find this particular amazing fiber, many worsted weight ribbon yarns would work beautifully with this ribbon shawl design.

Skill Level
BEGINNER

SIZE
One size

FINISHED MEASUREMENTS
48" (122 cm) at widest point by 48" (122 cm) long

MATERIALS
Nylon Ribbon by Looped Back (8 oz [229 g] skeins, each approx 400 yds [365 m]) Calypso, 1 skein or 400 yds [365 m] heavy worsted weight ribbon yarn

Size 13 (9 mm) needles, or size to obtain gauge

Size 17 (12.75 mm) or 19 (15 mm) needles for BO (optional)

Size H (5mm) crochet hook

GAUGE
2.5 sts and 4 rows = 1" (2.5 cm) over lace pattern using smaller needles

Refer to glossary on page 136 for: VDD and YO.

INSTRUCTIONS
Cast on 3 sts.

Following Holiday Scarf Chart, work YO increases as indicated to Row 42.

Rep Rows 31–42, working inc as indicated and repeating 12 center sts of chart as necessary between edge charts on either side.

Note: The 12-st repeat will end with st 6 in the last repeat of the chart before the left edge chart is worked.

When the 12 rows of the center repeat section are worked, repeat Rows 31–42 of the chart again. This time there will be an additional 12 sts as you work across the non-edge sts of the shawl.

Work until piece measures 48" (122 cm) long, or desired length. Work 4 rows of garter st, then BO all sts *very* loosely, using a larger needle if necessary.

Add fringe following instructions on page 115.

Steam-block.

See Blocking with Steam, page 112, for more information on blocking.

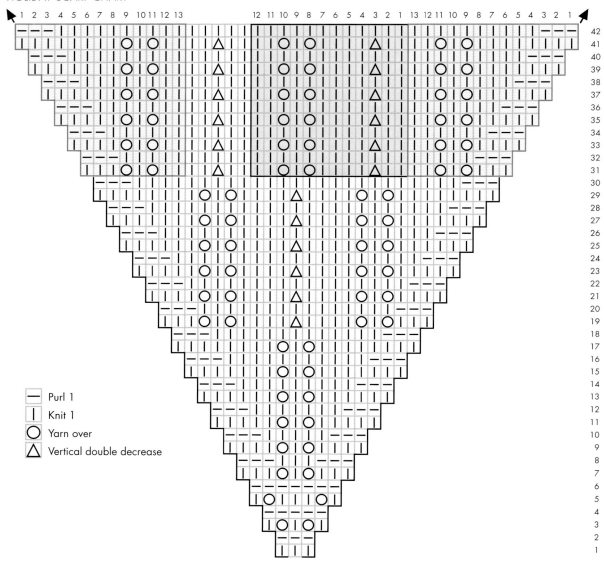

— Purl 1
| Knit 1
◯ Yarn over
△ Vertical double decrease

Basic Millinery Techniques

MEASURING HEADSIZE

The *headsize* is a millinery term for the part of the hat that sits just above the tips of the ear.

The headsize is generally the circumference of the head (measured just at the top of the ears) plus ½–1" (1.3–2.5 cm), depending on fit of the hat. Another vitally important measurement is the *ear-to-ear measurement*. Holding the measuring tape at the top of the left ear, pull the tape across the top of the head until it reaches the top of the right ear.

BLOCKING

The shape of the hat is achieved by blocking, wiring, and placement of the hatband.

The first step is blocking the hat. If you don't have a hat block handy in your size, you can make a soft block by shoving three or four dish towels into a pillowcase. Bunch them up until they're roughly your headsize, then twist the case around them. Set this ball of fabric into a mixing bowl slightly smaller than the ball itself and use this soft faux block to shape your hat.

STEP 1 Wet the crown of the hat (try not to get the brim too wet) by holding it under warm running water.

STEP 2 Gently squeeze out the excess water from the crown. Do not twist or wring the knitted fabric!

STEP 3 Place the hat on the hat block (it won't look very pretty at this stage!).

STEP 4 Pull the wet crown firmly over the hat block, being careful to pull the bottom edge of the brim evenly around the marking ribbon on the hat block.

STEP 5 Smooth the crown with your hands.

Working with twine or a tightly twisted yarn, it will not be necessary to pin the crown in place.

Allow the hat to dry *thoroughly* until it is completely dry to the touch. If desired, you may steam the hat instead of wetting it for a quicker block.

See Blocking with Steam, page 112, for more information on blocking.

MAKING THE HEADSIZE WIRE

STEP 1 Measure your head circumference.

STEP 2 Add 1½" (3 cm) to this measurement and cut a length of unsprung wire to this length.

STEP 3 Make a slipknot in the end of an 18" (45.5 cm) strand of heavyweight thread and tighten the knot around the end of the wire. Overlap the ends of the wire 1" (2.5 cm) and thoroughly wrap the heavyweight thread around the overlapped area, paying special attention to the cut ends of the wire. Wrap the overlap very tightly, but be careful not create a large bump by using too much thread in any one area. Finish off the thread by knotting it around the wire, then weaving it back under the wrapped strands.

ATTACHING THE HEADSIZE WIRE

Turn the hat inside out. At the point where the brim and the crown meet, there will be a noticeable ridge—the cast-on edge of the brim—this part of the hat is called the headsize.

Using a crochet hook and a single strand of yarn, crochet the headsize wire onto the headsize in the following manner:

Rest the headsize wire circle on top of the headsize edge and hold both gently together in the left hand.

STEP 1 Working beneath the headsize wire, push the crochet hook through the next stitch along the headsize edge.

STEP 2 Continuing to work beneath the headsize wire, pull a loop of the yarn back through the second stitch so that there are two loops on the crochet hook.

STEP 3 Now, working above the headsize wire, pull the strand of the yarn through both stitches on the crochet hook.

Repeat these three steps to single crochet completely around the headsize of the hat.

SPRINGING THE WIRE

Springing the wire is a term that means taking the natural tight coil out of the wire. When using millinery wire, it is necessary to "spring" the wire when working in large circumferences (wide hat brims). For smaller circumferences, it is not as important to spring the wire. Some milliners swear by springing, some feel it is entirely unnecessary. I find the necessity for springing the wire depends on the brim circumference desired. When springing the wire, be careful to move your thumb SLOWLY over the wire—move too fast and you'll give yourself a nasty wire burn!

MAKING THE BRIM WIRE

STEP 1 Lay the sprung milliner's wire around the outer edge of the brim so that the circumference of the wire is about 1" (2.5 cm) larger than the circumference of the hat brim.

STEP 2 Without cutting the wire, temporarily tape the wire circle closed at this point. Begin doubling the brim wire by working the excess wire around the established circumference and wrapping both thicknesses of wire together with button thread. Wraps should be about 1/8" (3 mm) apart and should be rather tight.

STEP 3 Continue working around the brim wire, adding to the heavyweight thread as necessary by tying on new 18" (45.5 cm) pieces (the knots will be covered when the hat is attached to the brim wire).

STEP 4 Work until the entire brim wire is doubled, then work 1" (2.5 cm) beyond the taped area (removing tape as you work past that part). Cut the wire. Wrap the heavyweight thread very tightly around the doubled ends of the wire, making sure to cover the cut ends as thoroughly as possible without creating a bulky bump. Finish off the thread by knotting it around the wire, then weaving it back under the wrapped strands. Working back around the brim, weave all thread ends into the wrapped strands in the same manner.

ATTACHING THE BRIM WIRE

When the brim wire is fastened into a circle, attach it to the outer brim of the hat by using a crochet hook and working in the following manner:

STEP 1 Hold the hat brim, right side up, in the left hand. Using a strand of yarn, make a loop on the crochet needle by pulling the strand through a stitch on the outer edge of the brim. Rest the wire circle on top of the brim and hold both in the left hand. Working beneath the wire, push the crochet hook through the next stitch along the brim edge.

STEP 2 Continuing to work beneath the wire, pull a loop of yarn back through the second stitch so that there are two loops on the crochet hook.

STEP 3 Working above the wire, pull the strand of yarn through both stitches on the crochet hook.

STEP 4 In order to completely cover the wire, and depending on the thickness of the yarn, it may be necessary to work more than one crocheted stitch into each knitted stitch along the wire.

The brim should attach to the wire tautly; it may be necessary to pull on the work as the attachment of the wire to the brim nears completion.

High Society

What makes a face look better than a beautiful brim to frame the features? Our mothers and grandmothers understood which hats looked best on them, what shape of brim or depth of crown would accentuate their beauty. A cloche (French for bell) hugs the head and gracefully spreads at the brim. It's very appealing on a variety of women, but it is most attractive on a long, oval face. Both hats in this book are worked from the headsize to the brim edge, then stitches are picked up at the cast-on and the crown is worked, decreasing to the tip.

Skill Level
INTERMEDIATE

See Basic Millinery Techniques, page 119, for tips on blocking and wiring a hat.

SIZE
Women's S (M, L)

FINISHED MEASUREMENTS
Headsize: 19 (21½, 23½)" (48.7 [55.1, 60.3] cm)

Crown Depth: 4 (5, 6)" (10.3 [12.8, 15.4] cm)

Outer Brim Circumference: 21 (24, 27)" (53.8 [61.5, 69.2] cm)

MATERIALS
Sunshine by Trendsetter (1¾ oz [50 g] balls each approx 95 yds [87 m], 75% viscose, 25% polyester), Antique Rose 61, 2 (2, 2) balls or 148 (171, 190) yds (135 [156, 173.50] m) worsted weight yarn

Size 5 (3.75 mm) circular needle, 16" (40.5 cm) long, or size to obtain gauge

See Circular Stress page 112 for thoughts on circular needle lengths.

Approx 3 yds (2.75 m) millinery wire (available at millinery supply stores, see Resources, page 134)

Size E/4 (3.75 mm) and F/5 (3.75 mm) crochet hooks

1 yd (1 m) 1" (3 mm) ribbon

Darning needle

Stich markers, including one in a contrasting color

Hat blocking form (See Blocking, page 119, for tips on making your own faux hat block.)

GAUGE
5.5 sts and 7 rows = 1" (2.5 cm) over Chart B and larger needles, after blocking

Note: Since you won't want to wire a swatch, follow this method to approximate the gauge you would get by blocking and wiring your hat: Cast on 20 sts and work in St st for 4" (10 cm), then bind off all sts. Press the swatch with an iron, pulling it taut in both directions. Allow the swatch to cool and rest, then measure for gauge.

Refer to glossary on page 136 for: K2togL, K2togR, K2tog Picot Bind-Off, VDD, and YO.

See page 47 Basic Crochet Techniques: SC

BRIM PATTERN

See Chart A if you prefer to work from charts.

ROWS 1 AND 3: Knit all sts.

ROWS 2 AND 4: Purl all sts.

ROW 5: K7, YO, k1, YO, k7.

ROWS 6, 8, AND 10: Knit.

ROW 7: K7, YO, k3, YO, k7.

ROW 9: K7, YO, k5, YO, k7.

Work Rows 1–10 once for pat.

CHART A
CLOCHE BRIM

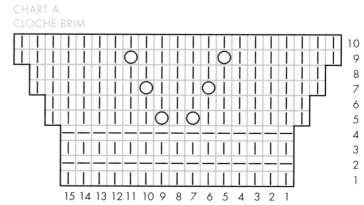

SIDEBAND PATTERN

See Chart B if you prefer to work from charts.

ROW 1: K1, YO, k4, k2togL, k1, YO, k1, k2togR, k4.

ROW 2 AND ALL EVEN-NUMBERED ROWS: Knit.

ROW 3: K2, YO, k4, k2togL, k1, YO, k1, k2togR, k3.

ROW 5: K3, YO, k4, k2togL, k1, YO, k1, k2togR, k2.

ROW 7: K4, YO, k4, k2togL, k1, YO, k1, k2togR, k1.

ROW 9: K5, YO, k4, k2togL, k1, YO, k1, k2togR.

ROW 11: K2togR, YO, k2togL, k7, k2togR, YO, k2togL.

ROW 13: K2togR, YO, k2togL, k5, k2togR, YO, k2togL.

ROW 15: K2togR, YO, k2togL, k3, k2togR, YO, k2togL.

ROW 17: K2togR, YO, k2togL, k1, k2togR, YO, k2togL.

ROW 19: K2togR, k3, k2togL.

ROW 21: K2togR, k1, k2togL.

ROW 23: VDD each group of 3 sts.

Repeat Rows 1–10 for sides of hat. Work Rows 11–23 once for crown shaping.

BRIM (WORKED FROM HEAD TO OUTER EDGE)

With circular needles, cast on 105 (120, 135) sts.

Knit 1 row, placing a marker every 15 sts to form 7 (8, 9) equal sections. Join, placing contrasting marker to note start of round.

Work all rows of Chart A once.

Using larger crochet hook, work k2tog picot bind-off, working 1 ch st between each BO st.

BEGIN CROWN

At inside edge of brim (cast-on edge), with circ needle, PU&K 105 (120, 135) sts, picking up 1 stitch for each original cast-on stitch. Place marker every 15 sts; markers should align with the points where markers were placed when knitting the brim.

HAT SIDES

Begin working Chart B.

Repeat the first 10 rows 3 (4, 4) times, or until hat measures 4 (5, 6)" (10 [12.5, 15] cm) from picked-up sts or is equal to the ear-to-ear measurement, see page 119.

Work Rows 11–23 once to create the tip shaping.

Break yarn, leaving an 8" (21 cm) tail and pull through the rem 8 sts.

Weave in end of yarn.

FINISHING

The hat is finished by blocking and inserting two wires: one where the brim meets the crown, and a second at the outer edge of the brim. See *Basic Millinery Tips*, page 119, for complete information on finishing the hat.

TRIM

After wiring the hat, SC using smaller crochet hook around entire brim with A. Weave in ends. Wrap ribbon around hat and tack in place as pictured.

CHART B
SIDEBAND PATTERN

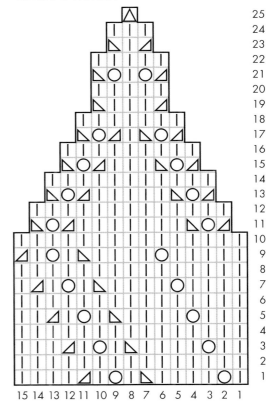

25
24
23
22
21
20
19
18
17
16
15
14
13
12
11
10
9
8
7
6
5
4
3
2
1

15 14 13 12 11 10 9 8 7 6 5 4 3 2 1

| Knit 1

O Yarn over

— Purl 1

△ Vertical double decrease

◣ Knit 2 together with a left slant

◢ Knit 2 together with a right slant

Gone with the Wind

In the 1950s, with the advent of widespread car ownership, hats began to shrink, and then they disappeared altogether. Hats just became too large to fit into a sedan, and the wide-brimmed oval hat, so necessary for walking to the bus or running errands without ruining the complexion, were no longer as needed. But times change, folks walk more, and we've become sensitive to the dangers of sun exposure. Make this lovely hat with a slight oval brim, sophisticated enough for a dressy afternoon wedding and casual enough for a stroll downtown for lunch!

Skill Level
ADVANCED

See Basic Millinery Techniques, page 119, for tips on blocking and wiring a hat.

SIZES

Headsize: 19 (21½, 23½)" (48.5 [55, 59.5] cm)

Crown Depth: 4 (5, 6)" (10.3 [12.5, 15] cm)

Outer Brim Circumference: 19¾ (23, 26¼)" (50 [58.5, 66.5] cm)

MATERIALS

A: Vintage Cotton by Karabella, (1¾ oz [50 g] balls, each approx 140 yds [128 m] per skein, 100% mercerized cotton), White 356, 2 (2, 2) balls or 246 (289, 326) yds (224.5 [263.5, 297.5] m) sportweight yarn

B: Vintage Cotton by Karabella, Black 310, 1 (1, 1) ball or 84 (100, 115) yds (80 [96, 110] m) sportweight yarn

C: Hug Snug® Seam Binding by Lawrence Schiff Silk Mills (Roll approx 100 yds [91 m], 100% woven rayon), Black, 1 roll or 50 (60, 70) yds (45 [54, 63] m) of ½" (13 mm) wide seam binding (available at most fabric stores) or rayon ribbon yarn

Size 5 (3.75 mm) circular needle, 16" (41 cm) long, or size to obtain gauge. See Circular Stress page 112 for

thoughts on circular needle lengths.

Approx 3 yds (2.75 m) millinery wire (available at all millinery supply stores, see Resources, page 134)

Size E/4 (3.75 mm) and F/5 (3.75 mm) crochet hooks

Stitch markers

Darning needle

Hat blocking form

See Blocking, page 119, for tips on making your own faux hat block.

GAUGE

5 sts and 7 rows = 1" (2.5 cm) over Chart B and larger needles, *after blocking*

Note: Since you won't want to wire a swatch, follow this method to approximate the gauge that you would get by blocking and wiring your hat: Cast on 20 sts and work in St st for 4" (10 cm), then bind off all sts. Press the swatch with an iron, pulling it tautly in both directions. Allow the swatch to cool and rest, then measure for gauge.

Refer to glossary on page 136 for: K2togL, K2togR, K2tog Picot Bind-Off, VDD, W&T, and YO.

BRIM PATTERN CHART

See Chart A if you prefer to work from charts.

ROW 1: Knit all sts.

ROWS 2 AND 4: Purl all sts.

ROW 3: K1, (k2togR, YO, k3) twice, k2togR, YO, k2.

ROW 5: K2, YO, k1, YO, k3, VDD, k3, YO, k1, YO, k2.

ROW 6 (AND ALL EVEN-NUMBERED ROWS THROUGH 18): Knit.

ROW 7: K3, YO, k3, k2togR, k1, k2togL, k3, YO, k3.

ROW 9: K3, YO, k3, k2togR, YO, k1, YO, k2togL, k3, YO, k3.

ROW 11: K6, k2togR, YO, k3, YO, k2togL, k6.

ROW 13: K2, YO, k3, k2togR, YO, k5, YO, k2togL, k3, YO, k2.

ROW 15: K1, YO, k3, k2togR, YO, k2togL, k5, k2togR, YO, k2togL, k3, YO, k1.

ROW 17: K3, YO, k1, k2togR, YO, k1, YO, k2togL, k3, k2togR, YO, k1, YO, k2togL, k1, YO, k3.

Work Rows 1–18 once for pattern.

SIDEBAND PATTERN

See Chart B if you prefer to work from charts.

ROWS 1 AND 3: With A, knit.

ROW 2: With B, (k1, sl 1); rep to end of round (if necessary, end k1).

ROWS 4 AND 6: With B, knit.

ROW 5: With A, (k1, sl 1); rep to end of round.

Rep Rows 1–6 to desired sideband depth.

TIP PATTERN

See Chart C if you prefer to work from charts.

ROW 7: K2togR, k1, YO, k3, VDD, k3, YO, k1, k2togL.

ROW 8 AND ALL EVEN-NUMBERED ROWS: Knit.

ROW 9: K2togR, k1, YO, k2, VDD, k2, YO, k1, k2togL.

ROW 11: K2togR, k1, YO, k1, VDD, k1, YO, k1, k2togL.

ROW 13: K2togR, k1, YO, VDD, YO, k1, k2togL.

ROW 15: K2togR, YO, VDD, YO, k2togL.

ROW 17: K1, VDD, k1.

ROW 19: VDD each group of 3 sts.

CHART A
OVAL BRIM

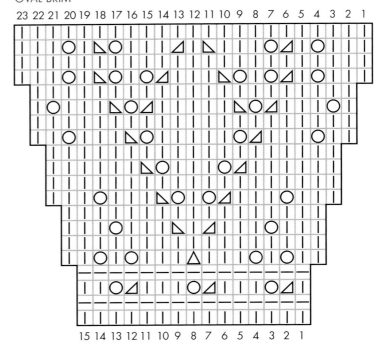

CHART B
OVAL SIDEBAND

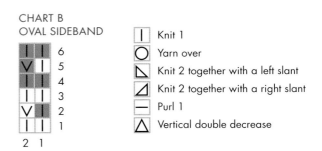

| | Knit 1
| O | Yarn over
| Knit 2 together with a left slant
| Knit 2 together with a right slant
| — | Purl 1
| Vertical double decrease

CHART C
OVAL TIP

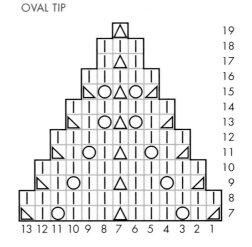

BRIM

With a single strand of A and circular needle, cast on 90 (105, 120) sts.

Knit 1 row, placing a marker every 15 sts to form 6 (7, 8) equal sections.

Work Rows 1 and 2 of Chart A (garter stitch) back and forth, then join, placing contrasting marker to note start of round.

Work Rows 3–20 of Chart B once—138 (161, 184) sts. For a round hat, work k2tog picot bind-off, working 1 ch st between each BO st. For an oval brim hat, continue to Oval Shaping.

OVAL SHORT-ROW SHAPING

LEFT EDGE OF HAT

NEXT ROUND: Knit 68 (80, 91), W&T.
NEXT ROW (WS): Purl 56 (64, 74), W&T.
NEXT ROW (RS): Working Row 19 of chart, work 44 (48, 56) in pat as est. *Only work dec when the corresponding YO can be worked, and vice versa.* W&T.
NEXT ROW (WS): Purl to 2 sts before last wrapped st, W&T.
NEXT ROW (RS): Cont in pat as est, working Row 19 of Chart A as directed above, work to 2 sts before last wrapped st, W&T.
Rep last 2 rows until 24 (32, 34) sts rem between wrapped sts, end with a WS row, continue purling back to start of round.

RIGHT EDGE OF HAT

Continuing to purl on WS, purl 68 (80, 91) past contrasting marker, W&T.
NEXT ROUND (RS): Working Row 19 of Chart A, work 56 (64, 74) in pat as est. *Only work dec when the corresponding YO can be worked, and vice versa.* W&T.
NEXT ROW (WS): Purl 44 (48, 56). W&T.
NEXT ROW (RS): Cont in pat as est, working Row 19 of Chart A as directed above, work to 2 sts before last wrapped st, W&T.
NEXT ROW (WS): Purl to 2 sts before last wrapped st, W&T.
Rep last 2 rows until 24 (32, 34) rem between wrapped sts, end with a RS row, continue working Round 19 as est to start of round.

With B, knit 1 round, slipping wraps up onto needle and working along with each wrapped st as you come to it.
NEXT ROUND: With B, (k8, YO) 17 (20, 23) times to end of round, end k2 (1, 0)—155 (181, 207) sts.
K2 rounds. BO loosely using a k2tog picot BO and larger crochet hook, if desired, chaining 1 st between each BO st.

BEGIN CROWN

At inside edge of brim (cast-on edge), pick up and knit 105 (120,135) sts, picking up 1 stitch for each original cast-on stitch.

HAT CROWN (SIDEBAND)

With B, work 2 rounds of garter st.
NEXT ROUND: (K1, k2togR, YO, k2); rep to end of round.
Work 2 rounds of garter st.
Inc 0 (1, 0) sts—90 (106, 120) sts.
With A, work 2 rounds of garter st.
With A and B, work the 6 rows of Chart B until sideband depth measures 4 (5, 6)" (10 [12.5,15] cm) from picked-up sts, ending with Row 3 of chart.
With A, work 2 rounds of garter st.
With B, work 2 rounds of garter st, then knit 2 rounds, then work 2 rounds of garter st. Dec 0 (1, 0) sts in last round—90 (105, 120) sts.

HAT CROWN (TIP)

NEXT ROUND: With A, knit, placing a marker every 15 sts.
Work Rows 7–19 of Chart C to create the tip shaping, 6 (7, 8) sts rem.
Note: Row 7 of Chart C shows 13 sts, but 15 total sts are used in each repeat; 2 sts are decreased in this row.
Break yarn, leaving an 8" (20.5 cm) tail and pull through the last 6 (7, 8) sts.
Weave in end.

FINISHING

The hat is finished by blocking and inserting two wires: one where the brim meets the crown, and a second at the outer edge of the brim.
See Basic Millinery Tips, page 119, for complete information on finishing the hat.

The Fit Is the Key

When we wear clothes that fit us, we look better. We can dream that we have a 22" (49.5 cm) waist, but dreaming won't get us a sweater or dress that is flattering. Clothes that are too tight make us look like we need to lose 15 pounds (6.8 kg) even if we're a perfect weight; clothes that are too loose have the same effect. Clothes that skim the body, not hug it, tend to be the most flattering.

It's vital that we're honest with ourselves—evaluating the parts of our figure we'd prefer to enhance and *using a tape measure* instead of relying on what we *think* our waist or bust measurement is!

Although the garment patterns have schematics with complete measurements, it's quite possible that your own measurements will span several sizes. Perhaps you have very long arms, but a short body; or your legs go on for days but your waist is a little thicker than you would like. In these cases, it's advisable to get out your pencil and make a note of which sleeve length, which body circumference, and which skirt length works best for you.

I've tried to include at least one place in each pattern where you can knit to a premeasured length, or to your *desired* length. Take advantage of these opportunities to create a handmade garment that is as flattering as possible!

Recommended Reading

✐ USED IN THE WRITING OF THIS BOOK

☆ A BOOK ALL KNITTERS SHOULD HAVE IN THEIR COLLECTION

✐ BIG GIRL KNITS
Jillian Moreno and Amy R. Singer
Potter Craft 2006

CLASSIC MILLINERY TECHNIQUES:
A COMPLETE GUIDE TO MAKING &
DESIGNING TODAY'S HATS
Ann Albrizio, Osnat Lustig, Ted Morrison
Lark Books 1998

CREATIVE KNITTING: A NEW ART FORM
Mary Walker Phillips
Van Nostrand Reinhold 1980

DOMINO KNITTING
Vivian Hoxbro
Interweave Press 2002

☆ ✐ ENCYCLOPEDIA OF KNITTING: A STEP-BY-
STEP VISUAL GUIDE WITH AN INSPIRATIONAL
GALLERY OF FINISHED WORKS
Leslie Stanfield, Melody Griffiths
Running Press 2000

✐ FASHION: A HISTORY FROM THE 18TH TO THE
20TH CENTURY, THE COLLECTION AT THE
KYOTO COSTUME INSTITUTE
Akikio Fukai, The Kyoto Costume Institute
Taschen 2005

FROM THE NECK UP: AN ILLUSTRATED GUIDE
TO HATMAKING
Denise Dreher
Madhatter Press 1981

✐ KNITTED EMBELLISHMENTS: 350 APPLIQUÉS,
BORDERS, CORDS AND MORE!
Nicky Epstein
Interweave Press 1999

✐ THE KNITTER'S BOOK OF FINISHING
TECHNIQUES
Nancie M. Wiseman
Martingale & Company 2002

THE KNITTER'S HANDY BOOK OF PATTERNS: BASIC DESIGNS IN MULTIPLE SIZES & GAUGES
Ann Budd
Interweave Press 2002

KNITTING FOR ANARCHISTS
Anna Zilboorg
Unicorn Books & Crafts 2002

KNITTING FOR DUMMIES
Pam Allen
John Wiley & Sons, Inc. 2002

KNITTING IN PLAIN ENGLISH
Maggie Righetti
St. Martins Press 1986

KNITTING IN THE OLD WAY: DESIGNS AND TECHNIQUES FROM ETHNIC SWEATERS— EXPANDED EDITION
Priscilla A. Gibson-Roberts
Nomad Press 2004

KNITTING LACE: A WORKSHOP WITH PATTERNS AND PROJECTS
Susanna Lewis
Taunton Press 1992

MARY THOMAS' KNITTING BOOK
Mary Thomas
Dover Publications 1972

NINETEENTH-CENTURY FASHION IN DETAIL
Lucy Johnston
Victoria and Albert Museum 2005

PATTERNS OF FASHION 2: ENGLISHWOMEN'S DRESSES AND THEIR CONSTRUCTION C. 1860-1940
Janet Arnold
Drama Publishers 1977
Victoria and Albert Museum

SOCKS SOAR ON TWO CIRCULAR NEEDLES
Cat Bordhi
Passing Paws Press 2001

THE CUT OF WOMEN'S CLOTHES
Norah Waugh
A Theatre Arts Book 1987

THE EDWARDIAN MODISTE: 85 AUTHENTIC PATTERNS WITH INSTRUCTIONS, FASHION PLATES, AND PERIOD SEWING TECHNIQUES
Frances Grimble
Lavolta Press 1997

THE KNITTER'S COMPANION
Vicki Square
Interweave Press 1996

VOGUE KNITTING: THE ULTIMATE KNITTING BOOK
Vogue Knitting
Sixth & Spring Books 2002

Resources

The materials used in this book are available at fine local crafts and yarn stores everywhere. I've provided this listing of retailers and wholesalers to help you find the closest supplier, or, where noted, to assist in finding an item that is a little more difficult to get.

YARN COMPANIES

ANNY BLATT
7796 Boardwalk
Brighton, MI 48116
www.annyblatt.com

ARTYARNS
39 Westmoreland Avenue
White Plains, NY 10606
www.artyarns.com

BERROCO
14 Elmdale Road
P.O. Box 367
Uxbridge, MA 01569-0367
www.berroco.com

CASCADE YARNS
PO Box 58168
Tukwilia, WA
www.cascadeyarns.com

CLASSIC ELITE YARNS
122 Western Avenue
Lowell, MA 01851
www.classicelite yarns.com

HABU TEXTILES
135 W. 29th Street
New York, NY 10001
www.habutextiles.com

KARABELLA
1201 Broadway
New York, NY 10001
www.karabellayarns.com

LANTERN MOON
7911 N.E. 33rd Drive, Suite 140
Portland, OR 97211
www.lanternmoon.com

LOOPED BACK
The beautiful hand-dyed ribbon yarn used to make Holiday (page 116) is currently available only at the Looped Back store or through their website.
810 Elmwood Avenue
Buffalo, NY 14222
www.loopedback.com

LORNA'S LACES
4229 N. Honore Street
Chicago, IL 60613
www.lornaslaces.net

LOUETF SALES/EUROFLAX
808 Commerce Park Drive
Ogdensburg, NY 13669
www.louet.com

PATONS YARN
320 Livingstone Avenue South
Listowel, ON N4W 3H3 Canada
www.patonsyarns.com

PLYMOUTH
P.O. Box 28
Bristol, PA 19007
www.plymouthyarn.com

SOUTH WEST TRADING COMPANY
918 South Park Lane, Suite 102
Tempe, AZ 85281
www.soysilk.com

TILLI TOMAS SPECIALTY YARNS
72 Woodland Road
Jamaica Plain, MA 02103
www.tillitomas.com

TRENDSETTER YARNS / LANE BORGOSESIA
16745 Saticoy Street, Suite #101
Van Nuys, CA 91406
www.trendsetteryarns.com

YARN SOURCE
Passion, the silk yarn featured in Now, Voyager
(page 68), is manufactured exclusively for
Lambikins Hideaway. You can purchase it through
their website or at their shop.
Lambikins Hideaway
217 South B Street
Hamilton, OH 45013
www.lambikinshideaway.com

NONYARN RESOURCES
I have found the following shops to be extremely
helpful for hard to find or one-of-a-kind items.

SCHIFF RIBBON /
HUG SNUG SEAM BINDING
79 Madison Avenue
New York, NY 10016
www.schiffribbons.com

SCHOOL PRODUCTS
For specialty needles and books.
1201 Broadway, 3rd Floor
New York, NY 10001
www.schoolproducts.com

JUDITH M HATS & MILLINERY SUPPLY
104 S. Detroit Street
La Grange, IN 46761-1806
www.judithm.com

STEINLAUF & STOLLER, INC.
For notions and fasteners of all sorts, even
seam binding.
239 West 39th Street
New York, NY 10018
www.steinlaufandstoller.com

MOKUBA
For fine Japanese ribbon.
55 W. 39th Street
New York, NY 10018
www.mokubany.com

TENDER BUTTONS
For antique and specialty buttons.
143 E. 62nd Street
New York, NY 10021

COLONIAL NEEDLE, INC.
Excellent straight and circular needles.
74 Westmoreland Ave
White Plains, NY 10606
www.colonialneedle.com

Stitch Glossary and Chart Symbol Key

When a symbol is used in a chart in this book to describe a stitch or technique, it is displayed with the stitch description. Please consult a reference on knitting techniques (see Recommended Reading) for detailed instructions on basic and advanced knitting techniques. In places the terms *public* and *private* are used interchangeably with the terms *right* and *wrong* to describe the working side of the fabric.

3-NEEDLE BO—THREE-NEEDLE BIND-OFF (ALSO CALLED BINDING OFF TOGETHER)

STEP 1 Place the two pieces on knitting needles so the right sides of each piece are facing each other with the needles parallel.

STEP 2 Insert a third needle one size larger through the leading edge of the first stitch on each needle (knitwise).

STEP 3 Knit these stitches together as one, leaving 1 stitch on the right-hand needle.

STEP 4 Repeat Steps 2 and 3.

BO
Bind off.

CIRC
Circular.

C4L OR C4F—CABLE 4 LEFT OR CABLE 4 FRONT

 Cable 4 stitches with Left Twist (also known as Cable 4 Front), slip 2 stitches, knit 2 sts, bring slipped stitches to front of work and knit them.

C4R OR C4B—CABLE 4 RIGHT OR CABLE 4 BACK

 Cable 4 stitches with Right Twist (also known as Cable 4 Back), slip 2 stitches, knit 2 stitches, bring slipped stitches to back of work and knit them.

CCO—CABLE CAST-ON
Adjust work so that all stitches are on the left-hand needle. Slip needle between first and second sts on left-hand needle and pull loop through to front. Slip this loop onto the left-hand needle, twisting it clockwise. Repeat, each time using new st as new first stitch on left-hand needle.

DEC
Decrease.

DKSS—DOUBLE KNIT SLIPPED STITCH

Right-Side Row: Knit 1, with yarn in front slip 1, knit 1, work to last 3 stitches, knit 1, with yarn in front slip 1, knit 1.

Wrong-Side Row: With yarn in front slip 1, knit 1, with yarn in front slip 1, work to last 3 stitches, with yarn in front slip 1, knit 1, with yarn in front slip 1.

Note: On right-side rows "yif" means yarn to the right side of the work. On wrong-side rows "yif" means yarn to the wrong side of the work.

EST

Establish(ed).

FOLL

Following, follows.

FRINGE

Using a crochet hook and folding each fringe piece or group of fringes in half, pull the center of a single piece of fringe through the cast-on or bound-off stitch, then pull the ends of the fringe through the loop, securing the fringe to the edge of the piece. Steam-block, combing the fringe so it is straight, and cut along the bottom edges to even the fringe. Add a dab of Fray-Chek if the fiber unravels easily.

GARTER ST

On Straights—Right side and wrong side: Knit all stitches.

In the Round—Round 1: Knit all stitches.

Round 2: Purl all stitches.

I-BOBBLE

I devised this bobble as an alternative to the traditional bobble. For a very firm bobble, wrap the yarn around the base of the finished bobble a couple of times before working the next stitch.

Knit 3 stitches into next stitch. Slip these 3 stitches back to left-hand needle and knit.

Knit 2 into first stitch, knit 1, knit 2 into last stitch. Slip these 5 stitches back to left-hand needle and knit. Repeat for a larger bobble.

Knit 1, vertical double decrease, knit 1. Slip stitches back to left-hand needle and knit.

Repeat last step until 3 stitches remain, VDD last 3 stitches.

I-CORD

Cast 3 stitches onto a double-pointed or circular needle. (Slide these stitches to the opposite end of the needle and knit them; Do *not* turn needle.) Repeat until cord is desired length.

I-CORD BO—I-CORD BIND OFF

Cast on 2 stitches at the start of row using Cable Cast-On. (Knit 2, knit 2 together left. Slip 3 stitches from right-hand needle back onto left-hand needle. Pull the yarn taut across back of work.) Repeat across work until 3 stitches remain, knit 3 together left.

I-CORD CAST-ON

The row immediately above this cast-on can be very loose. Practice it on your swatch before attempting it on the actual garment.

Cast on 3 stitches. Knit these 3 stitches and slip them back onto the left-hand needle. Next row: Make 1 increase by knitting 2 stitches into first stitch, knit 2. (Slip last 3 stitches from right-hand needle to left-hand needle, knit 2 stitches into first stitch, knit 2); repeat until you have cast on the stitches required plus 2 additional stitches. Slip last 3 stitches from right-hand needle to left-hand needle, knit 2 together, knit 1. Slip last 2 stitches from right-hand needle to left-hand needle, knit 2 together.

I-CORD HORIZONTAL STRIPE

(Cast on 1 stitch using Cable Cast-On, keep the new stitch on your right-hand needle. Knit 2, knit 2 together left. Slip 3 stitches from right-hand needle back onto the left-hand needle.) Repeat across work until all stitches are worked.

INC

Increase.

K1

| | Create a stitch by inserting the needle through the stitch from the front to the back, wrapping yarn around the needle and pulling loop through.

K2, P2 RIB (MULTIPLE OF 4 STS)

Right Side: Knit 2, purl 2.
Wrong Side: Knit 2, purl 2.

K2TOG PICOT BO—KNIT 2 TOGETHER PICOT BIND-OFF

This can be easily worked with a crochet hook in lieu of the left-hand needle. To add picot chain stitches to the k2tog BO, work as follows:

Knit 2 together left, (slip the stitch created back onto the left needle, [knit this stitch, then slip the stitch just created back onto the left-hand needle]), repeat as many times as required—1 repeat for each picot chain.

(Slip the stitch back onto left-hand needle and knit together with the next stitch as knit 2 together left.) Repeat to the end of the row, draw fiber tail through the last loop.

K2TOGL—KNIT 2 TOGETHER WITH A LEFT SLANT

In a traditional knitting pattern, a left-slanting 2-stitch decrease will be written as SSK, K2tog-TBL, or S1 K1 PSSO. I prefer to call these decreases K2togL to indicate that they have a left slant.

K2TOGR—KNIT 2 TOGETHER WITH A RIGHT SLANT

Traditionally, decreases that slant to the right are called k2tog. I prefer to call them k2togR to indicate that they have a right slant.

K3TOGR—KNIT 3 TOGETHER WITH A RIGHT SLANT

As with k2togR, knit 3 stitches together so they slant to the right.

K3TOGL—KNIT 3 TOGETHER WITH A LEFT SLANT

As with k2togL, knit 3 stitches together so they slant to the left.

LONG-TAIL CAST-ON

Also known as a 2-strand cast-on, this is a method of casting on whereby 2 strands are used and the finished cast-on consists of 1 row of cast on sts and 1 row of

knitting. When using a long tail cast-on, you'll begin your first row on the *wrong side* of the work.

STEP 1 Place a slipknot several inches into a strand of yarn (roughly 1" [2.5 cm] for each stitch to be cast on). Place the slipknot on a knitting needle and hold the needle in your right hand. Be sure to keep the tail toward you and the live end of the yarn away from you.

STEP 2 With the needle in your right hand, slip your left thumb and index finger between the two strands of yarn and separate them. Hold both strands of yarn securely in your left hand.

STEP 3 Spread your thumb and index finger and turn your palm upward. Touch the tip of your needle to your palm and slide the needle up your thumb, under the yarn.

STEP 4 Move the tip of the needle toward your index finger and grab the strand that is wrapped around that finger. Return to the thumb and slide the tip of the needle back down the thumb toward the palm.

STEP 5 Allow the loop around your thumb to slip off, separating the two strands to tighten the cast-on stitch just created.

M1—MAKE ONE STITCH

 There are several ways to make a stitch. I call this right slanting increase the "grandma" increase. When worked on the wrong side as a "grandma purl," this increase will slant to the left when viewed from the public side.
Insert needle into stitch *below* next stitch on the left-hand needle, pull a loop of yarn through, creating a stitch, then work the stitch immediately above. Slip stitch off the left-hand needle.

M1—MAKE ONE STITCH WITH LEFT SLANT

 If you need to make a left-slanting increase on the public side, this is one way to do so.
Lift stitch below last stitch knit onto left-hand needle, knit this st.

PM

Place marker.

P1—PURL 1

 Create a stitch by inserting the needle through the stitch from the back to the front, wrapping yarn around the needle and pulling loop back through.

P2TOGL—PURL 2 TOGETHER WITH A LEFT SLANT

 Purl 2 stitches together so they slant to the right when viewed from right side of the work.

P2TOGR—PURL 2 TOGETHER WITH A RIGHT SLANT

 Purl 2 stitches together so that they slant to the left when viewed from right side of the work (also known as p2tog-tbl).

PAT
Pattern.

PROVISIONAL CAST ON

Generally worked with a piece of scrap or waste yarn, a provisional cast on allows the knitter to remove the cast on row and pick up the newly live stitches in the first row and work them.

There are many excellent provisional cast ons in use, but one of the easiest utilizes a crochet hook.

STEP 1 With a piece of waste yarn and a crochet hook slighly larger than the knitting needle, create a crochet chain, one chain for each cast on stitch.

STEP 2 Insert the knitting needle into the back loop of each chain.

Use the loops on the needle as your cast on row. When you want to release the first row and re-use them, carefully undo the last chain stitch, then pull the waste yarn to pull out the crochet chain and release the first row of knitting. Pick up these stitches and work as directed.

PU&K—PICK UP AND KNIT

Insert needle into fabric, wrap yarn around tip of needle and draw through fabric.

QDD—QUAD DOUBLE DECREASE

Slip 3 stitches as if to knit 3 together with a right slant, knit 2 together with a left slant, pass slipped stitches over stitch just worked—decrease of 4 stitches.

REM
Remaining, remain.

REV ST ST—REVERSE STOCKING OR STOCKINETTE STITCH

On straight needles—Row 1: Purl. Row 2: Knit. On circular needles: Purl every round.

SL ST—SLIP STITCH

Slip next stitch to the right-hand needle without working it.

SL ST WYIF—SLIP STITCH WITH YARN IN FRONT (ALSO KNOWN AS WYIF SL1)

Bring yarn to front, slip next stitch to the right-hand needle without working it, move yarn to back.

ST ST—STOCKING OR STOCKINETTE STITCH

On straight needles: (Right Side) Knit. (Wrong Side) Purl.
On circular needles: Knit every round.

TWISTED CORD

Measure a length of yarn 4 times longer than desired length of final twisted cord. Fold the strand in half and make a slipknot at the cut ends. Pass the slipknot over a doorknob and stand far enough away that the yarn hangs in midair and does not touch the ground.

Slip a crochet hook into the loop you are holding in your hand and pull the cord taut so that the hook rests perpendicular to your fingers, allowing the hook to slip between your middle and pointer finger.

Begin turning the hook—similar to the way that the propeller on a toy airplane twists a rubber band—to twist the strands of yarn. Continue twisting until the yarn is quite taut and evenly twisted. When relaxed slightly, the twisted yarn should want to kink up. Still holding one end of the yarn in your left hand, with your right hand pinch the twisted strand midway between yourself and the doorknob.

Bring the ends of the yarn together by moving toward the doorknob, but *do not let go of the middle of the twisted yarn*. When the piece is folded in half, you can release the middle of the cord. You will notice the yarn twisting around itself, forming a plied cord. Still holding tightly to the looped end, loosen the slipknot end from the doorknob and tie both ends together. Run your finger between the cords to even out the twists if necessary.

TWISTED FLOAT LEFT SLANT

 2 stitches are shown in the symbol. This will twist the strands of yarn.

Working on the wrong side and keeping strands to right side of work, with A, knit 1, drop strand, (bring strand of B under hanging strand of A, with B, knit 1, bring strand of A under strand of B, with A, knit 1); repeat to last stitch, with B knit 1.

Working a round of twisted float left slant will untwist the strands that have spiraled around each other in the twisted float right slant round.

TWISTED FLOAT RIGHT SLANT

 2 stitches are shown in the symbol. This will twist the strands of yarn.

Working on wrong side, keeping strands to right side of work, with A, knit 1, drop strand, (bring a strand of B over a hanging strand of A, with B knit 1, bring a strand of A over strand of B, with A, knit 1); repeat to last stitch, with B, knit 1.

TW1—TWIST 1 STITCH

 When working this stitch, insert the needle into the stitch so that the stitch twists (tightens) as it is worked. This is used to close yarn overs and to create twisted rib (also known as k1tbl).

VDD—VERTICAL DOUBLE DECREASE

 A decrease that slants neither to the left nor the right is a *vertical* decrease and will consist of an *odd* number of stitches. Other vertical decreases could include QDD (quad double decrease), which would consist of 5 stitches reducing to 1 stitch, a decrease of 4 stitches total.

Slip 2 stitches as if to work knit 2 together, knit 1, pass slipped stitches over knit stitch.

W&T—WRAP AND TURN

 Slip next stitch to right-hand needle, wrap yarn around the stitch, and return to left-hand needle. Turn work and begin working back in the opposite direction from the previous row.

WYIB—WITH YARN IN BACK

Move the yarn away from you to the back of the work.

Note: Back may not be the wrong side of the work.

WYIF—WITH YARN IN FRONT

Move the yarn toward you for the next step.

Note: Front may not be the right side of the work.

YO—YARN OVER

A yarn over is sometimes called a Yarn Forward (YF) in British patterns. To make a yarn over, wrap the yarn around the needle *in the same direction as it was wrapped in the previous stitch*.

YYK—YO YO KNIT

Slip right-hand needle into stitch as if to knit, wrap yarn twice around right-hand needle.
Next row: Only work the first loop in this stitch, allowing second yarn over to drop, creating an extra-long stitch.

Sample and Test Knitters

ADINA ALEXANDER
The Heiress—Embroidered Cardigan

KATHLEEN CATLETT
Saratoga—Banded Tank

KENNY CHUA
Gigi—Wavy Lace Scarf

CAROL DIDIER
Casablanca—Lace Panel Corset
Silk Stockings—Silk Long Stockings

DOUG IBERG
Two for the Road—Double Layer Pullover

JANN JONES
Some Like It Hot—Long Opera Gloves

LAUREN LAX
A Room with a View—Lace Peplum Surplice

SARA LINQUIST
All About Eve—Ribbon Wrap Skirt

LAURA MESSINA
Adam's Rib—Chesterfield Jacket

JESSIE O'CONNOR
Vertigo—Egyptian Striped Scarf

LAURA PRESCOTT
The Bishop's Wife—1930s Shirtwaist

PAULETTE RAND
A Streetcar Named Desire—Pink Tulip Cardigan

SCOTT SIMPSON
Gigi—Wavy Lace Scarf

JULIE SPARKS
Charade—Lattice Lace Surplice Top

MARNI SUSSMAN
Gigi—Wavy Lace Scarf

MIRIAM TEGELS
West Side Story—Ruffled Skirt

GRUMPERINA
Cleopatra—Egyptian Chevron Dress

CRYSTAL WELCH
Now, Voyager—Matelasse Skirt

Index